Indra and Armando
Miami, November 1985

CLOSET FULL OF COKE

A DIARY OF A TEENAGE DRUG QUEEN

INDRA SENA

Imagine if the mistakes you made as a teenager threatened you the rest of your life? I made mortal enemies in my short career as a drug lord and I've lived a certain way because of that. But as a lover of stories, I felt this story demanded telling. And although twenty-five years has softened the pain, it has not erased the well of memories.

In truth, I'd rather not speak of it at all, and in life I almost never do. Everything told here happened. This is a memoir. Events happened in the order presented and while I was the age listed on the diary entries. Much has been left out for focus, flow, and brevity. Time was slightly condensed. I've changed the names of people and towns. I've also left out as many innocent bystanders as possible because this is a book about criminals.

After years spent writing this book I still have no idea why I made the choices I did as a teenager, or why I seemed to posses so much criminal finesse. I deeply regret those choices and that I harmed so many people in my wake.

Books saved my life both as a child and an adult. That's also why I wrote this book. Glimpsing into a hidden subculture can be entertaining. It is also cautionary: a tale of playing with danger, and the inevitable consequences.

It is one of the oldest stories on earth. Drug dealers and criminals refer to it often themselves by simply saying: if you gonna play, you gots to pay.

PART ONE

One

Mesc: A misnomer for tiny, hallucinogenic, purple pills. Mesc is short for the word mescaline, a reference to peyote cactus. The pills do not contain peyote. They are made from low-potency LSD and fillers.

Buy: A wholesale purchase of drugs by a drug dealer.

"You looking for something?"

I was standing on the porch of my dealer's house, anxiously ringing the doorbell. I turned around to see a thirtysomething Latino man standing behind me. I hadn't heard him come up the porch steps. He was sleek, and his dark eyes were captivating. His remarkably handsome face was framed by glossy black hair brushed neatly back. He appeared regal in a full-length gray wool coat topped with a flowing black scarf, and shiny black leather shoes.

"I'm here to see Jamal." I pushed my hands deep into the pockets of my black leather jacket.

1

"No one is home." He spoke slowly in heavily accented English. "You are looking for something, *sí?* I can help you." The cadence of his voice had a slight hypnotic effect on me.

He kept his dark eyes locked on me. I turned and walked across the decaying porch planks of the sprawling Victorian house to peer into the kitchen window. It did seem unusually quiet.

I was there to make a buy. I'd been hitchhiking to this house for two years, since I was thirteen, buying mesc to sell to my suburban classmates. The Lincoln brothers—all six of them—lived, turned tricks, and dealt drugs here. I often sat in the shadows of the living room silently watching the freak show; businessmen in smart suits arriving to pay for sex with black men wearing full drag, teenage girl streetwalkers in miniskirts buying pills, and hollow-eyed junkies sweating and panting for heroin.

When I came to make a buy, I would sit on the red velvet couch smoking Marlboros while the oldest, Jamal, counted out dozens of tiny purple pills on the coffee table.

"Here you go, girlfriend," he'd say while tossing me a miniature plastic bag containing the pills, "now you gots to pay your daddy." Then he'd flash a wide, disarming grin while flipping the blue feather boa he often wore over his shoulder.

I'd take wads of bills out of my purse that were mostly singles (the lunch money my classmates paid me with) and hand them to him.

When I'd stand and announce that I was leaving, he'd jump up and give me a juicy kiss goodbye. He always flirted with me, but not in a serious way. It was more like he was teasing me.

He'd say something like, "Girl, you so fine. We should hang out together some night."

I knew he was joking, but I still had a crush on him. He was tall and stately, and he looked like an athlete with his muscular physique. I thought he was gorgeous.

2

Living as an unsupervised teenager, I stumbled into drug dealing. At first, I bought my drugs from high school seniors I partied with, and then re-sold them to my peers in middle school for a profit. But then I met Jamal at a liquor store near his house where I went to buy cheap wine with fake ID. He was charming. We formed an instant bond, and when he took me to his house full of lava lamps, colored beaded curtains, and velvet furniture, I thought it was the coolest place I'd ever seen. I began hitchhiking there regularly to buy all of my drugs from him.

The Lincoln brothers' house was always full of people, mostly hookers and junkies. I found them intriguing, especially the girl hookers who were my age. I became friends with two of them. They called themselves Spicy and BJ, and they were always forking their hard-earned cash over to their boyfriends—wanna be pimps with needle bruises covering their scrawny arms.

Spicy and BJ told me countless stories of sex for profit. Sex with toothless old men, or with men so fat they had to climb on top of them by stepping on a folding chair. And sex with shoe-fetishists who masturbated while the girls pranced around rank hotel rooms in high heels. They were always bumming cigarettes off me, and asking men for spare change as we walked down the street together.

I couldn't quite understand their choice to hook. As a dealer, there was no sex with sleazy men for a twenty-dollar bill, and no pimp to take that bill away. I lived like royalty. Everyone wanted to be my friend. I was phoned constantly, sought out between classes by kids camping in front of my locker, saved the best seat on the school bus, and stalked by the Jonesers; those ghosts who think of nothing but getting high.

When I focused on something, I tended to excel. I thought about being a lawyer, or a teacher, but I was afraid I would never fit into the normal world. When I spoke of college, my mother, Joan, sarcastically called me a dreamer. She suggested I clean houses instead.

The stranger extended a gloved hand towards me. "Come with me," he said, and flashed a movie star smile. "I'm Armando."

I took his hand and walked down the porch steps holding it, teetering slightly on the stiletto heels of my black suede boots. When we reached the pavement, I jerked my hand away.

"Where are you taking me?"

"For a ride."

Taking a deep breath, I stared blankly at him. "No, I'm sorry, I can't. I don't know you."

"Ah, but I know you. I saw you leaving here once, and I asked Jamal about you. You are the *gringa* who comes from the country to buy mesc." He placed his hand on my arm, and I knew I was going with him.

"Come with me to pick some up and I will give you the best deal," he said.

I followed him along the sidewalk. I thought he was the most charming man I'd ever met. I flirted with him, smiling and twisting a long dark curl with my finger while we walked.

I suspected Armando was Jamal's supplier. Going over your dealer's head to his dealer is considered a loathsome crime of loyalty. I loved Jamal, but my ambition had long outweighed my loyalty; I had gone over my dealer's head before. Besides, I didn't go looking for Jamal's supplier. I just got lucky.

Armando stopped walking. He stepped off the curb and opened the driver side door of a brown El Camino, and then pulled the beige front seat forward. He motioned for me to get in. A typical Hispanic car, I thought. The Virgin Mary statue glued to the dashboard completed the stereotype.

4

Sliding into the backseat, I noticed a girl up front holding a baby. Her shiny black hair, pulled tightly back with an elastic band, fell to her waist. She looked about my age.

"This is Lourdes, she does not speak too much English."

"*Hola, mucho gusto.*" I fumbled to speak the tiny bit of Spanish I knew.

She replied in rapid-fire Spanish.

I interrupted her. "*Un poquito.*"

"The little you speak is good," Armando said. "I'll teach you. Do not learn from her, she is Puerto Rican. She butchers my language."

"Is that your baby?"

"Yes. José. He is one year."

Armando started the car, and then jerked it quickly away from the curb forcing us all to lurch. The unexpected slide across the seat sent me slamming into the door. As we drove, Lourdes clutched her baby to her chest. I held onto the headrest in front of me.

He soon careened onto the interstate and floored the gas, weaving in and out of narrow lanes, passing cars on both sides without signaling, and honking his horn in frustration. He yelled and cursed in Spanish while angrily tailgating every car in his path.

I had never seen anyone drive like this before. A man I once talked to in a bar told me people in other countries drive really crazy. He was from Egypt, and he said there were no traffic lights there. Maybe Armando had only just come to America?

"Where are we going?" I hoped talking to him would distract him, maybe slow him down. It only made things worse as he looked over his shoulder to talk to me without braking.

"114th Street."

"You mean the city?"

"No, Manhattan."

"That is the city, and it's over two hours away! Why are we going there?"

"To get mesc. That's what you want, sí?"

"Yeah, but I didn't plan on being away for hours."

I had hitchhiked to Jamal's straight from school. My sister Seely, who was only thirteen, was home alone with no one to watch her. Our mother had been sleeping at her new boyfriend's house almost every night. We had friends who came over to drink and drug with us daily, so she probably had company, but I didn't want to disappear on her for hours.

"I'm gonna give it to you cheap, *muchacha.*

Half the price you pay the Lincoln brothers. I'm getting you a hundred hits for seventy dollars."

I was thrilled. I immediately began calculating the increased profits in my head. But dealers, like poker players, must always hide their true feelings. I remained stoic. He glanced at my expressionless face in the rearview mirror. I glared at him. "If you don't fucking kill us, *cabrón.* You drive like a crazy man, slow down." I looked over his shoulder at the speedometer. It was punched to eighty-five. "Slow the fuck down or let me outta this car!"

Armando laughed. "Okay, *chica,* I'll try, but you are mine now."

His gentle bullying annoyed me. I would never be his — or anyone's, especially not for a crummy handful of drugs, not even for a million dollars.

I sat back and rummaged through my purse. It contained a small notebook where I kept my drug books and wrote poems, and a small silk bag with pearl-colored rosaries my grandmother had given me. I also carried two makeup cases. One was a black case housing cherry red lipstick, black eyeliner, powder, and a battery powered lighted mirror, and the other was a pink case that functioned as a stash bag with marijuana, rolling papers, and small glass joint holder inside.

6

"Can I smoke pot?" I asked.

"Sure, it is okay. Just relax." Armando switched on a Spanish pop station and blasted the tinny music.

I rolled a perfect joint. I placed it in the cigarette holder and lit it, deeply inhaling the thick smoke. No one wanted any so I smoked alone, occasionally leaning forward to survey the speedometer.

When we reached the city, it was night.

"Armando, where are we?"

"Spanish Harlem."

He parallel parked along the curb, and then jumped out of the car telling us to lock the doors. I felt nervous as I watched him walk to the corner, turn, and vanish.

I had heard of Harlem, as in the Harlem Globetrotters. Other than that, it meant nothing to me. At home, I hung out in what was called "Spanish Town." Spanish Harlem looked a lot like it with its painted brick townhouses, and tiny stores lining the streets with signs advertising *Lotería* and *Licor de malta* along with flashing red and yellow lights circling the windows.

Lourdes and I struggled to converse, then politely gave up. I wished I spoke Spanish so I could ask her about Puerto Rico. Instead, I passed the time by watching the people walking by. There were girls swathed in rabbit fur with high, tight ponytails and huge gold hoop earrings, and young men in parkas walking in small groups talking animatedly. Occasionally I'd see a solitary figure walking briskly, seemingly coaxed by the cold wind.

I was drawn to Latin culture: the exotic sounding Spanish words spoken so rapidly, the spicy food, the garish décor, and the candles with the Saints on them. When I was twelve, I liked a boy named Manny Rodriguez. I gave him my number and he called me while I was out. My mother answered the phone and while taking a message, she asked his name.

"Don't you know you can't date spicks?" She began yelling as soon as I came through the front door.

"Why not?" I asked.

"'Cause, you go wich your own kind. You can't date any boys unless they're the same as you."

I went out with Manny anyway. I liked brown skin, melodic accents, and jet-black hair.

Armando finally returned with small bags full of steaming hot food. "These are *empanadas*, we eat them in Colombia all the time. You have never tasted anything so good." We ate the hot yellow pastries filled with spiced beef out of grease-stained paper bags.

I said that I needed to call my sister. Armando nodded and then drove slowly down the street, pulling over when he spotted a phone booth. He offered me some change. I jumped out of the car clutching a handful of dimes and was soon pushing dirty buttons with my black leather gloves.

"Seely? Were you asleep?" She sounded groggy.

"Nah, I'm just fucked up." She then burst into laughter. "Where the fuck are you, you never came home after school?"

"I had to leave town, I'll be back around eleven. Are you okay? Did ma call?"

"I'm alright, just hangin' out with Jack. Ma never called tonight."

"Cool." I was relieved she was with Jack, her boyfriend for almost a year.

"Where are you, sissy?" Seely always called me by the same nickname our father called his sister.

"I'm doing business ... working, ya know. I'll tell you later."

Seely was my biggest fan. She often bragged at school about being my sister. I felt responsible for her and even though I was often mean to her, she was the only person I trusted with my secrets.

When I got back into the car, Armando asked me where I lived.

"Farmingville."

"Where's that?"

"About ten miles from Southbridge."

"Oh, sí. No *hay problema*, I will drive you home. *Aquí.*" He tossed me a tiny packet containing more mesc than I had ever seen. I pulled the money out of my wallet and gave it to him.

"You gotta pen, muchacha?"

I pulled out a pen along with my trusty notebook.

"Here is my number. From now on you call me, sí?"

"Sí."

The ride home was quiet. Lourdes rarely spoke, though occasionally she murmured to Armando in Spanish, and he answered almost as softly. I understood nothing they said, but it sounded like music.

Armando looked at me often in the rearview mirror. Sometimes, I met his gaze and held it for a moment. His raven eyes made my heart race. Maybe I saw my future in them, a future more glamorous than I'd ever dreamed, and more horrible than I'd ever feared.

Two

Seely and I exchanged fearful glances as we sat down at the kitchen table. Joan sat across from us, biting her nails and frowning. Her brown eyes looked vacant.

"I'm moving in with Harry, and I can't take youse there. He don't like kids; he never had 'em. Youse live here for a few months until we decide where you go. Your father said youse can go live there." She looked down, smoothing the red-checkered vinyl tablecloth with worn hands.

"We have never lived with Daddy before, and we've already been to four schools. Plus, you know Leona hates us." I said.

Leona was my father's third wife. They had been married sixteen months, and she was pregnant with their second child. She chain-smoked two packs of Newports a day, and her bleached-blonde hair, premature wrinkles, and tanning cream tinted skin made her look closer to forty than twenty-nine.

"I fucking tell you, look at me, I'm a fucking nut," she would say with a laugh. "I've got two fucking cigarettes lit, one in each goddamn hand!"

Leona's kitchen was a place where Catholic alcoholics gathered around the table to trash their neighbors. Zack, my father, liked to sit there while stoned and debate them. They were Leona's friends, mostly unmarried women with multiple kids. They spent endless hours debating issues like who really killed Jesus, and whether there was a conspiracy that made welfare unfairly distributed. Listening to them made my head hurt. I would fantasize of strangling Leona, who was always the loudest.

Joan, on the other hand, was a simple-minded yeller. She took her work and money stress out on Seely and me, throwing raging fits over a spilled glass of milk, or slapping me hard for reading too much. On the plus side, she ignored the fact that I was dating a twenty-three year old man with a full beard, and she let me use my fake ID to drink in bars with her.

No way did I want to leave Joan's house—a mix of random violence and unchecked freedom—to live at Leona's. I preferred the harpy I knew.

We sat in tense silence. I focused on watching the snow falling outside the kitchen window. I finally looked over at Seely. Her sky-blue eyes were clouded with tears. She looked so young and small.

"Move out after we graduate high school, Joan," I said. My jaw was tight with rage. I'd have to switch schools if Joan moved to another district, and I was tired of being the new girl. If Joan made this move, I would never finish high school.

"I can't live my life for youse two. I'm very old and this could be my last chance for love. You'll understand when you're my age." Her raven hair fell in waves around her smooth-skinned face. She was thirty-three.

I lost it and screamed, "You're so selfish. You're not a mother!"

Joan rose from her chair. She was a large woman who outweighed me by at least a hundred pounds. She leaned across the table and slapped my face hard. The cool sting, along with her handprint on my cheek, lasted for hours.

She got up and began to bustle about, preparing for her evening departure. She started washing dishes as if nothing had happened. "Kids, youse can finish the school year." Her tone was conciliatory, as if finishing a school year was a kindness being offered.

Seely was still silent, though she looked at me with questioning eyes.

I started crying, and then began yelling at Joan from my seat at the table. "How can you do this to us? You're so fucked up. I hate you, you selfish bitch!"

Joan turned around from the sink and looked at me with fury. I jumped up and ran toward my bedroom. Joan chased me, trying to grab my long hair, but I beat her to my room and locked the door.

I slid down onto the floor of my room, curled into a ball, and sobbed.

Renegades raised me. My father Zack grew pot in our tomato garden and stored it in a towering red Snap-on toolbox. He sold it to his many friends as they "stopped by." Joan cleaned houses and offices while helping herself to the cleaning products she found there. Windex, Palmolive dish liquid, Comet, as well as paper towels and toilet paper were put in a trash bag and disguised as garbage. Instead of being dropped in the can on the way out, the bags full of goodies were put in her car and brought home.

My parents railed against the government and authority. The IRS wanted to steal your money, the cops were pigs, and the landlord was a son of a bitch. Joan dodged bill collectors by training me to lie to them on the phone and tell them she wasn't home. Her house cleaning money was unreported cash, none of which had to be given to "those bastards," while Zack was nicknamed The Weasel for his crafty way of mooching loans of cash from a friend's wallet while simultaneously smoking all the weed he had just sold the guy.

A construction worker and mechanic by trade, Zack also took almost any odd job. I helped him carry washing machines and refrigerators up multiple flights of stairs, handed him wrenches and pliers while he rebuilt car engines, went with him on visits to his friends where cash and goods were exchanged, and drove his large van perfectly long before I was old enough to have a driver's license.

I was obsessed with solving the money dilemma that plagued our family. When I was eleven, I answered a classified ad in the back of a comic book and started selling flower seeds door-to-door. I quickly learned the pleasure of having money. By the time I was thirteen, I was continually creating schemes to get money. I shoplifted, mostly candy, and sold my stolen booty to classmates. But the money was paltry. I needed to make more.

I dreamed of phone service without interruption, an apartment without the constant, nagging fear of eviction, and a car without rust holes on the floor you could see the road through. I also wanted freedom, the kind my parents, with all the marriages and babies, always lamented they didn't have—freedom from burdens, from responsibilities, and from bill collectors.

The day after Joan's announcement, I hitchhiked after school to Spanish Town, my beloved section of Southbridge. I called Armando from a corner phone booth, and he told me to meet him at a bar. I walked five blocks to a tiny glass storefront with blackened windows and music blaring from inside. It was dark. Armando sat at the bar watching soccer. I sat down on the stool next to him. He asked what I wanted. I said I didn't know. I usually drank vodka straight from the bottle. In bars I drank rum and coke, but I really didn't like either.

"Strawberry Hill is my favorite wine," I said. It was fruity, sweet, and ninety-nine cents a bottle at the *Liquor y Bebidas Tienda*.

He spoke in Spanish to the bartender, who I watched add frozen strawberries to a small blender. Next, using both hands, he tipped two bottles of clear liquor over the berries. He added a squeeze of lime before blending the ingredients into a kind of spiked Slurpee. He placed the icy pink drink in front of me and I sipped it through a straw.

"It is a daiquiri," said Armando.

"*Gracias*. Listen, my mother wants to move and leave Seely and me. I don't know what to do."

"My mother left too, when I was a young boy."

"Who raised you?"

"Nobody." He tugged on the gold Saint Christopher medallion he always wore.

"Did you go to school?"

"No. I farmed until I was sixteen. Then I joined the Colombian Navy."

"Really? Did you learn how to fight at sea?"

"No, no," he laughed, "I cleaned a lot, the work was ... no good. Then I ran off at a port in Florida."

"And then you came to New York?"

"*Sí*."

"What did you do then?"

Armando turned and spoke in Spanish to the bartender. He placed two shot glasses full of clear liquid in front of us.

"What's this?"

"Peach Schnapps, you'll like it. *Salud!*"

"Salud! What are we toasting?"

"Freedom. Yours. Mine. No one needs a mama, you must believe that."

We tossed the shots back. The burn of the liquor was familiar, but the aftertaste was sweet peach. The blasting juke box played Latin pop, the kind I heard everywhere around here—pulsing in darkened bars, blasting from open windows of brick row houses, drifting out of car windows, and playing in tiny corner stores on cheap radios.

The men staring at the silenced television screamed out occasionally during soccer plays. I finished my daiquiri in silence while Armando watched the game. I tapped on his arm, and he broke out of a seeming trance.

"I gotta go." I jumped off of my barstool and pulled my purse over my shoulder.

"Sí. Do not worry, chica. It will all be *fácil* ... means, um, good. *Bueno.*" He hugged me tightly for a second and then gave me a small push towards the door.

Lightheaded from the drinks, I stumbled. Armando chuckled but when I turned around to protest, he was back to staring at the television.

When I opened the door of the bar, it was dark outside. Dark for hitchhiking, I thought. But once I walked to the main road, I had a ride in minutes.

Three

Rush (isobutyl nitrite): a pale yellow flammable liquid that is inhaled illicitly and named for the ensuing "head rush" felt after inhaling.

Front: Drugs given to a dealer by a supplier without exchanging money with a verbal agreement that they will be paid for after they are sold.

I stuck my thumb out while walking backwards on the roadside shoulder hitching a ride to Southbridge. I was missing a morning geometry test, but I had other priorities. My supplies of mesc and speed were depleted.

A fat, balding man stopped his car and asked where I was going.

"Corner of Morgan and Main."

"Get in, girlie."

I jumped into his Buick's front seat. "I'm going to work."

He offered me a cigarette while eyeing my blue angora sweater. It was fancy; I had shoplifted it from a swanky department store.

"What, are you a secretary or something?"

"Yeah, I am."

"Well, maybe you should get yourself a sugar daddy. A girl pretty as you shouldn't need to hitchhike."

I ignored his lame proposition and we both smoked in silence. I asked him to let me out the moment we hit Southbridge, even though it meant walking an extra ten blocks. He pinched my ass as I got out of his car, but I didn't even look back. Typical.

Armando opened the door of his house shirtless, wiping sleep from his eyes.

"Muchacha, why so early?"

I followed him inside and sat on the couch. "I needed to see you before school, *lo siento*."

"No problema, what do you need?"

I asked him for a hundred hits of mesc and fifty hits of speed. Speed was slang for the pink and white caffeine pills I also sold.

"*Mira*, let me give you extra, say, double."

"But I don't have enough cash for that. Why did you call me Mira?"

He smiled. "Mira, means, um, look. The extra stuff, it's on the front."

It was a gesture of trust.

"Really? I'll even up soon, I promise. I gotta run though, practically everyone in my school is waiting for me. Gracias!"

"*De nada*," he said.

I kissed his cheek and taking my drugs, I dashed out the door.

I was so excited. After only two months of weekly visits, Armando was now fronting to me. I could now extend that credit to other dealers. I would make way more profit selling to another a dealer as opposed to a user. It was a step up the dealer's ladder.

I walked four blocks back to the main road after I left Armando's and stuck my thumb out. A young man pulled over in a silver Peugeot.

"Where you going?" He spoke so softly it was hard to hear him.

"King High."

He didn't speak the entire ride. I was creeped out by his silence and relieved when he finally dropped me at my school thirty minutes later. I raced into the cafeteria ready for lunchtime sales. I went to my regular table, located in the farthest corner of the atrium. Protected from unseen approaches on two sides by walls, kids sat there with me by invitation only.

"Where've you been?" Chrissy asked as I sat down next to her.

Chrissy was tall and lean, like a boy, with huge green eyes. She introduced me to stealing cars and shoplifting when we were thirteen, and we'd been inseparable ever since. We both were largely unsupervised and both criminally bent. Though once indoctrinated, I was clearly the most corrupt.

"I had to see my guy. I'm totally stocked."

"I asked the Colero sisters to do lookout."

"Cool, I'll hook them up."

The Colero sisters were the toughest girls in school and they were always eager to assist me. I reached over and handed them a few hits of mesc and a joint. They sat at the end of the table as guards. If anyone walked towards us, they drummed Led Zeppelin songs by slapping the hard top of the table. This was our cue to be cool and hide whatever we were doing.

Chrissy and I sat in the middle of the table like royalty holding court. A succession of people took turns sitting across from us. They were mostly guys, druggies with Pink Floyd T-shirts who were into tripping, though the occasional girl sat down asking for speed pills for her diet.

The money I made dealing bought us pizza, vodka, Rush, beer, pot, and cigarettes. We also hung out in bars using fake IDs, over-tipping, drinking rum and cokes, and playing Pac-Man for hours.

"We will now observe a moment of silence for Angela," said the principal on a mild spring afternoon, sounding somber on the classroom loudspeaker. My classmate Angela, a beautiful girl with huge doll eyes and blonde ringlets, had vanished while hitchhiking almost two weeks ago. Today, we were told, her dead body was found in the nearby woods.

After the announcement, I cut out of class and walked to the corner store a block from my school. Every local paper headline screamed something lurid about Angela. "Cheerleader Raped and Murdered." "Girl's Tortured Body Found." "Police Say Missing Girl Was Strangled." I bought three papers and sat reading them on the sidewalk in front of the store. All I could think about was poor Angela alone with no one to help her, out in the woods with only trees to witness her struggle.

Chrissy found me hunched over the newspapers.

"Why are you crying?" she asked.

"Angela, she—"

"You didn't even know her. Plus, you hate cheerleaders. She was a fucking cheerleader!"

"But I did know her, we were in chorus together. She was really nice, and what happened to her … it's just so horrible."

"Fuck those bitches, let's go get high."

We went to the small store next to the deli run by a Pakistani man who spoke little English. It was a head shop with bongs, pipes, roach clips, posters, black lights, incense and small glass vials of Rush. I tossed a crumpled ten-dollar bill on the counter and pointed to the Rush. Chrissy and I went behind the store with the small brown bottle. We took turns quickly twisting open the black lid and inhaling the rich chemical smell before slamming the lid back down.

Later that night, at Sam's Bar and Grill, we were eating pizza and drinking beer with Chrissy's boyfriend Jeff, and Paul, a man from our neighborhood who we ran into at the pool table. I had admired him from afar for years. He looked like Peter Frampton with his long rock star blonde locks and bangs.

"We're going to play another game," Chrissy said as she got up and headed towards the pool table with Jeff. "Are you guys coming?"

"I'm gonna smoke first," I said.

Paul didn't respond. He remained seated across the table from me, silently looking at me. I was nervously playing with my fork.

"So, beautiful, what grade are you in?"

"Tenth."

"Do you want another beer?"

"Yeah, sure."

Paul scooped up our beer glasses and walked across the room, placing them on the bar for refills. I was smitten. It didn't matter to me that he was twenty-five, in fact, I preferred men to boys my age.

Since I was fourteen, I'd been fooling around with men in their twenties. There was the older brother of a classmate, a neighbor, and a guy who worked at a gas station who I met when I refueled a temporarily stolen car. I never had sex with them, but we spent hours petting in their cars. They'd secretly pick me up around the corner from my house and we'd drive to secluded cornfields. It was like a visit to an opium den. I would lie in a dreamy state of carnal pleasure for hours while they kissed and stroked my naked body. The feeling was better than any drug I knew. I would stumble home late at night, stoned on teenage hormones, pot, and cheap wine.

Paul sat down next to me after fetching our beer, looking at me with flashing eyes and a mischievous smile.

"What? Is something wrong?" I asked.

"Oh no, there's nothing wrong. I just never noticed before how pretty you are. I love your eyes."

I smiled and took a sip of my Budweiser. "I need a cigarette, I'm going out back to smoke."

"I'll go with you, if you want," he said as if on cue since I was trying to get him to follow me. I could have lit up right there at the table, but I wanted to be alone with him.

Outside Paul lit my Marlboro. When I dropped my hand and blew out smoke, he leaned over and kissed me.

We walked away from the bar holding hands, heading for a trail that cut through the woods and led back to our housing development. Halfway down the trail Paul stopped, put his arms around my waist, and pulled me close. Then he began kissing me passionately.

He stopped at one point and said, "Damn, lady, who taught you to kiss like that?"

"I don't know." I didn't mention the other men I'd been with.

"Well, you're the best kisser I've ever met."

We made out for what felt like hours, then we started to get cold. It was late. Paul said we should head home so we continued down the trail arm in arm towards my house.

At my door, I invited him in. "My mother is at her boyfriend's, it's cool."

"No, princess, I have to leave you here. Believe me, I want to come in, I just can't."

"Okay." I had no idea why he couldn't come in, but I didn't ask.

Paul kissed me on my front step, then scurried off calling out, "Good-night, Miss Luscious."

Miss Luscious? I wasn't sure what it meant, but I smiled at his pet name.

The next day I called Armando instead of going to school.

"Mira, can you come pick me up at my house?"

"*Por qué?* Why?"

I told him about Angela, about how she died and how scared it made me to hitchhike. I told him I never wanted to hitch a ride again.

"I need to go have a few drinks at Hector's, I just don't want to be at school today."

Speaking softly he offered his condolences, and then offered to give me a ride anywhere, anytime.

"I will come get you now and go with you. We're *amigos, correcto?* I'm not going to let anything happen to you."

Four

Seely and I were living alone for a few months with no problems. If our mother showed up unexpectedly, we snuck our few guests out the window. She was never there more than an hour and when she left, the party returned.

But then we got the idea to have a huge, blowout party. We spent the better part of a month planning it.

During the bash, the phone was accidentally left off the hook. Joan tried to call for hours and couldn't get through. She showed up and began screaming for everyone to get the fuck out of her house. Kids raced out of doors and jumped out of ground floor windows. I shoved Chrissy and the others I was smoking pot with in my bedroom into my closet. Joan burst into my room, chasing and slapping me. I scurried around trying to dodge the blows.

"Pack your bags, you're coming with me!"

When she left my room, I opened my closet door to talk to my friends. "You guys just stay here until after we're gone, it'll be cool."

Chrissy glanced at a red welt on my arm. "Yeah, and I'm gonna rob your cunt mother's house on the way out."

Joan took Seely and me to Harry's. She assigned us each a room then left to return to the bar she'd been at with him. Late that night they came home and began to brawl on the front lawn, which soon brought the state troopers. Seely came to my bedroom door sniffling and scared. I let her sleep in my bed.

The next day I clandestinely called Chrissy. "Chris, you gotta help me keep things going. I gotta keep my business going, no matter what."

"No problem," she said. "I got a list of orders for you, I'll come tonight."

"Cool, but come to my window in back of the house. I don't want you getting caught here. This scumbag my mother's with will call the cops."

Chrissy came while Joan and Harry were at the bar, so we smoked a joint at the window and hung out awhile.

"What are you gonna do, girlfriend?"

"Here, take these and sell them." I passed her a plastic bag full of mesc. "Bring back the cash as soon as you can, I need money. I'm gonna run away."

Later that evening, I told Seely we had to run away and she agreed. The next night I came to her bedroom with a small duffle bag. My mother and Harry were passed out drunk.

"Where are we going, Sissy?"

"Anywhere we want," I answered, dangling Harry's car keys in my hand. We climbed out her window and slipped into his car.

"Shit, I can't drive a stick." I pounded my first on the dashboard in frustration. "Motherfucker!"

"I can," Seely said.

We switched seats, and she put the car in neutral so it rolled silently down the steep driveway. At the bottom, she started it up and took off, stepping on the clutch and shifting gears.

"How the fuck do you know how to drive a stick?"

"Daddy showed me."

We drank vodka from a bottle I had stolen from Harry's house while we smoked a joint and blasted a Beastie Boys tape. Seely drove us around uneventfully for about an hour, and then a police car pulled up behind us at a traffic light. It was past three in the morning. I panicked, but Seely confidently shifted gears preparing to take off. The car abruptly stalled. Two more failed attempts followed. I was sure the cop would turn his lights on any second, but suddenly the engine engaged, and we zipped off. Seely and I laughed.

Sometime around dawn, Seely started insisting we return the car. "We'll go to jail. You know that dick will press charges."

"Yeah, I guess so. But maybe we should just drive it into the river and leave it there."

"Sissy, no, we'll be in worse trouble. If we put it back, he won't even know it was gone."

We returned the car near dawn and then walked eight blocks to a diner. I called a friend of mine named James, who lived with his friend Tom. They were both high school dropouts. James said we could spend the day at their place while Tom's parents were at work. We were totally exhausted, but we managed to walk another ten blocks from the diner to their house. I smoked some pot with them, and we all passed out for a few hours.

In the afternoon the four of us sprawled on the living room floor smoking a joint while listening to Bowie sing about Ziggy's inevitable demise. The phone sitting on the end table rang, and Tom pulled on the long, twisty cord until the receiver landed on his chest.

"Hello? What? Well … yeah … yeah … hold on."

He handed the phone to Seely.

It turned out to be Zack. He had apparently been making calls all morning and had gotten Tom's number from some rat. I was shocked at my father's resourcefulness. I grabbed the phone from Seely and hung it up. He called back. I commanded everyone to let it ring. Seely started crying, saying we were being mean to Zack. I finally let her answer and the stupid girl agreed to let him come and get her.

I screamed at her for telling him where we were, and I yelled at Tom for admitting we were there.

No one spoke. I ran around the room gathering my stuff into my bag. Grabbing my shoes, I sat on the arm of the couch and pulled them on.

I glared at Seely and the boys. "Are you all fucking retarded?"

"Where else are we gonna go, sis?" Seely's voice quivered with tears. "We have to go with Daddy."

"Well I'm not going with anyone. I'm gonna get an apartment, my own apartment, where no one can tell me what to do. Armando will help me, he said he would."

"I can't go, sissy, I can't. I'm sorry, I'm afraid."

"Of what?"

"I don't know, but I have a bad feeling and I want to go with Daddy."

Seely seemed to be decades younger than me, and it sort of made sense because my father always said I was born forty.

The phone rang again. Tom answered, and then thrust the phone towards me. "It's your father."

I took the phone, hung it up, and unplugged it from the jack.

I hugged Seely goodbye and left before Zack arrived. I had James drop me off a few blocks from Armando's apartment and begged him to lie about where he'd left me. I had to stay in hiding until I was sixteen, when it was legal for me to live on my own. And that would be in less than two months.

Lourdes answered the door sporting two black eyes. I was taken aback, but said nothing. She served Armando and me iced tea in silence and then disappeared. I sat down on the cramped living room floor and let the draft from the window fan hit me. The living room was drab. The tan sectional was weathered, and its square bulk took up almost the entire room. There were no photos and no knick-knacks, just plain white walls.

I told Armando everything that had happened.

"Okay, you call my landlord, sí? He has twenty buildings or more. Tell him I sent you. Oh, and you say you are married."

"Married?"

"Sí. He won't ask you questions."

"Why should I tell him that?"

"*Por qué te lo dije.*"

"What?"

"Oh, sorry, um ... because I tell you to."

When I think of pimps, I think of the TV show Baretta. Huge feathered hat, long white fur coat, glittery eyewear, you know, Rooster. Armando was a different kind of pimp. He was luminous and he easily won admiration from both males and females. Contradictions seemed to work in his favor. He was charming yet caustic, vulnerable yet tough. Then, there were those limpid eyes. But Armando wouldn't waste his time pimping a girl for sex; there was little money in that. My brain was the organ he planned to profit from.

On a narrow one-way street in the heart of Spanish Town, I found an apartment. It was up two winding flights of stairs in an old Victorian house. The bedroom, living room and kitchen all had the same pale yellow linoleum on the floor. Tall windows made it sunny and bright. Rent was two hundred dollars per month, all utilities included. I handed the landlord cash. He didn't ask me a single question.

Armando came over a few days after I moved in and offered me a blue Chevy Nova he got for seventy-five dollars. I offered him money, but he tossed me the keys and said, "*No te preocupes,* no worries."

I got new customers, mostly Puerto Rican guys from my hood. My apartment became a local hangout. Occasionally Armando stopped by but he wouldn't stay if I had visitors. He would simply send a brief, withering glance around the room and then leave.

As soon as my phone was hooked up, I called Seely at my father's house.

"Leona is an evil bitch," she said. "I hate it here."

"I told you."

"I know, but what am I gonna do?"

"Put our father on the phone."

Zack got on and I fought with him about how Seely was being treated. He countered with arguments of how impossible Seely was to live with, how she was hyperactive and driving him nuts. Then he started talking about how I was wrecking my life, so I hung up on him.

Five

One hot afternoon, I was housecleaning when my doorbell rang. I pushed a button that released the lock on the front door downstairs, and then opened my kitchen door. Armando bounded up the stairs and came through my door grinning.

"I love seeing you domestic. Look at you—you are a housewife. Me, I love that. You could be my *criada*."

I was wearing a short lemon yellow terrycloth dress over matching shorts and holding a mop in one hand. With no makeup on and my hair high up in a ponytail, I did look pretty domestic.

"I'm no housewife, *maricón!*"

Laughing at my chutzpah, he sat down on the couch while glancing at the gold watch shining on his dark wrist. I knew so little about him. He didn't reveal much, and he hated questions. Sometimes I wondered if Armando was even his name. His dressy button-up white shirt, gray linen pants and polished leather shoes made him look out of place compared to my typical visitors' garb: sneakers, jeans, and T-shirts with band names like Judas Priest on them.

"Chica, you and me are about to get really rich."

"We are?"

"Sí."

"You mean by getting more customers?"

"No. I've met some people, from my country. They can get us *cocaína*."

"Cocaine? You're crazy. I've never even met anyone who does that. It's like some Hollywood thing that stars do. I've never even seen it."

"Yeah, *mi hija*, it is the next big thing. *Vas a ver*, you'll see. Think about it. How much *dinero* do you want? I plan to be rich. Us together, we would make millions."

"Millions?" I didn't believe him. Who were we gonna sell coke to?

Six

September 1984

Age 16

Shotgun: A pot smoking practice in which one person inhales a hit of pot, and then exhales the smoke into another person's mouth as that person inhales.

It was the third week of the new school year. Mrs. Reilley, my English teacher, was lecturing the class on Ethan Frome. English was my favorite subject, and books were my favorite pastime. The last few weeks in her class had been thrilling.

In the middle of the lecture Mr. Lewis, my guidance counselor, knocked on the classroom door. He apologized to my teacher for interrupting and then he summoned me, telling me to bring my books. Following him through the empty halls, I plied him with questions.

"We'll talk in my office," he said, while he limped along the corridor. A stroke had left him dragging one foot slightly behind the other. He stopped at my locker.

"Why are we here?"

"Empty your locker."

"But why?"

"You're being expelled."

With textbooks stuffed into my book bag and gym clothes draped over my arm, I sat across from Mr. Lewis at his desk, first protesting, then crying, and finally pleading.

"Look, you don't live in this district anymore, and neither does your mother," he said.

"How do you know?"

"Another mother called to make a complaint."

"What did she say?"

"She said it was unfair. If her kids can't come to this school because they live in Southbridge, then why should you? You have to go to Southbridge High."

"But this is already my fourth school. Please, give me an exception. I can't start over again. Just let me finish high school here."

Then he said something that stopped my tears, and my protests, for good.

"We know about you ... about what you do, and I just can't help you. The principal wants you gone."

I slunk out of his office, and then out of King High forever.

I called Zack as soon as I got home. "Daddy? I got expelled today and I think it might be a sign for me to leave school and go full-time as a dealer."

"Are you out of your fucking mind? What will you do without an education?"

"You don't have one and I'll make more money than you ever did, and I won't leave my kids and be broke all the time!"

34

I knew he'd be upset. I had only called to hurt him anyway, because I was mad at him over Seely. Last week, his wife had accused her of stealing money from her wallet. Zack sided with Leona, who I knew was lying, because Seely told me everything. Zack yelled at Seely, hitting and then grounding her. In response, Seely ran away and stupidly went to Joan's. She ended up in a detention home, where I could only call her at certain hours. It was like jail. She was only fourteen, and you had to be sixteen to live without a guardian in New York State.

I flipped on General Hospital and rolled a joint. My phone rang a few times, but I ignored it.

Around midnight, my favorite new customer knocked on my living room window. Enrique, a swarthy Puerto Rican man, always came and left by way of the black iron fire escape. I slid open the tall window and he climbed inside, kissing my hand as he stepped off of the sill.

We sat down on the couch together. It was our first time alone, and I was nervous. Neither of us had ever hid our attraction for the other.

"'Rique, you ever do coke?" I said.

"*Qué?*" He packed a pipe with weed, then lit it and passed it to me.

"You know, cocaína."

"Shit no. I sniffed heroin a few times, and that stuff fucked me up. *Por qué?*"

I shrugged. "Just wondering. People say it's the next big thing."

"Chica, will you give me a shotgun?"

As I blew the smoke into his mouth, we started kissing, but a few minutes later, I pulled away from him.

"We have to stop now."

"Por qué, chica?"

"You just need to go now."

"Because of him? That *viejo* that watches over you?"

"No, come on. It's just that … I don't know. I should work tonight."

"Fine, *no hay problema.*" He slipped out the window, barely saying goodbye.

I wanted to be with him, but I was afraid of Armando dropping in. He said getting romantically involved with customers was a bad business practice, so I promised I wouldn't mess around with my customers. Occasionally, I fooled around with boys from school, but that was after they snuck me into their bedrooms. There was no way Armando could find out about them.

That was another rush I loved—doing things forbidden to me by a man who thought he controlled me—but no way did I want to get caught.

Seven

October 1984

Age 16

CO: Short for correction officer, which is another name for a prison guard.

After my expulsion from school, I mainly stayed in Southbridge. I even got all of my groceries at the bodega. While shopping, I met Jane, a white girl from my block. She was sixteen and living with a thirty-year old black man. Her entire family had disowned her. I invited her over to hang out and go to the mall with me.

In Macy's, Jane shoplifted a pair of shoes by putting on a new pair at the display and leaving her old ones behind. I didn't even know she'd done it until we were leaving the store and the in-house detective confronted us. We ignored him and walked towards my car. We would have made it, but a police patrol car making the rounds came by just at that moment. The cop jumped out of his car and in minutes determined that Jane possessed stolen shoes.

I denied involvement and argued nonstop with the young police officer, refusing to hand my pocketbook over. Finally, he tore my purse from me and forced my hands behind my back. First he put me in handcuffs, and then he put me into the back of his squad car. After cuffing Jane he put her in back with me. He jumped in the front, and as he drove he called on his radio to tell the station he was bringing in suspects.

"So, miss, what's inside your purse that you don't want me to find?" The cop had turned around to talk to me while we waited at a traffic light.

"Nothing."

He turned back towards the traffic.

"Girl, tell him," whispered Jane, and when she did, he looked back again at us and smiled.

"Listen to your friend. I can help you."

I had ten hits of purple mesc in a mint candy tin. Luckily, most of my stash was at home. I decided to play "dumb girl."

"Well, I don't know what it is exactly. This guy that stands on my corner sometimes, he gave it to me. He said it makes you laugh."

"You don't know? And you were going to take them?"

"I guess, maybe. I don't know."

"Are you nuts? Is he a drug dealer?"

"I don't know. I don't really know him."

"Where does he live?"

"I've only seen him on the corner, he stands there sometimes."

I marveled at my ability to craft lies so well on my feet. Joan had trained me to lie and to evade questions when talking to bill collectors, but now I was under arrest and being grilled by a policeman, not lying on the phone to a lady from the electric company. I hadn't read a handbook on being a master criminal, but somehow I knew exactly what to do. I knew how to talk, seeming to cooperate, and give no information. This knowledge seemed otherworldly to me, as if ghosts of criminals past were whispering it into my ear.

At the police station, we were turned over to officers who asked us our addresses, snapped our mug shots, and took our fingers and rolled them onto an ink pad, then onto a sheet of paper, creating a perfect map of each tip.

We were escorted to a police car. Two officers told us we were going to see the judge. No one said a word about the drugs I had on me. My arresting officer must have thrown them out or kept them because I was never charged with possessing them, but they disappeared from my purse, tin and all.

"What'd you do, raid a playground?" The grumpy, white-haired judge asked the cops. We were in his chamber, which was an office attached to his house. He then complained we interrupted his dinner. In small towns like the one the mall was in, the single judge was always on call.

"Well, what do you girls have to say for yourselves?" He looked sternly at Jane and me.

I started explaining that there was a mix up. He waved his hand in the air signaling me to shut up.

"Both of you are charged with shoplifting. Neither of you lives at home with your parents. I think some time in jail will straighten you out." He then declared that we be brought to jail without bail.

Normally for a small crime like shoplifting, you are simply released with a date set for your hearing.

"Without bail?" I started to tremble. "Please, your honor, my mother threw me out and—"

"Well maybe now you'll learn to be good, won't you?"

"But we're not murderers!"

"One more word little girl, and I'll add contempt of court on top of this petty theft charge."

We were handcuffed again, and placed back in the police car. While the officers drove us to the county jail, they teased us about how the girls there were rough, and how we'd probably come out lezzies. Jane and I were silent. I focused on how I might get out of my handcuffs, Houdini-style. My wrist bones are very small, but no amount of twisting would free my hands.

At the jail, the cops handed us over to two uniformed men. Without speaking to us, each one extended a single hand and tightly gripped our upper arm. They then pulled us along a long, brightly lit corridor. We soon learned that they were COs, and they would now be our keepers. We shuffled past a group of them sitting in a small room and they laughed at us.

"Stupid kids," one said.

They stopped in front of an empty cell. One of them took out his keys, which were attached by a metal cord to his belt. He unlocked and then opened the door of bars.

"Okay girls, time to go into the holding tank." We both hesitated, and one of them gave me a shove. I stumbled into the cell, and Jane followed. They locked us in and walked away. After silently glancing at each other, we sat down on metal benches attached to the wall. We didn't talk, but we both hung our heads and sniveled. An hour later two female guards came and opened the cell door.

"Come on ladies!"

We shuffled towards them and they escorted us across the hall to a tiny room with no windows. They ordered us to take off all of our clothes.

Jane and I stood there naked and freezing. They put on latex gloves and ordered us to squat. They searched our ears and hair, running their fingers along our scalps, and then cavity searched us, confirming there was no contraband hidden up our cooches.

"Put all of your possessions, clothes, and shoes into these bags." They held open black plastic bags. "You'll get it all back when you leave. You'll wear prison-issued sweat suits until you get approved clothes brought in. You'll be given a list of what is allowed and what is contraband." They gave us grey sweat suits and slip-on white canvas shoes. "Now, put these on, we going to put you on the tier."

"What they get you for?" A Puerto Rican woman with a huge mane of frizzy hair asked us as we entered a rectangular cage.

"Shoplifting."

A group of women had formed around us. They all laughed.

"'I'm Janina," said the woman with the hair. She came close and started to stroke my hair. "*Tan linda*, so shiny. My chulo would love you."

"Is Chulo your boyfriend?" I asked.

All the women laughed again and one said, "Chulo means pimp, gringa!"

The prisoners in jail were not scary at all. They were actually very friendly. Almost all of them were prostitutes.

On the other hand, the COs were terrifying. They barked orders at us and called us stupid if we asked questions. They purposely slammed the iron cage doors when opening and closing them, even in the middle of the night. The racket of the crashing metal was nerve-racking.

At night, all the prisoners were locked alone in tiny individual cells. I lay on my narrow wall mounted metal bed, watching roaches crawling along the crayon yellow walls, thinking about the young cop who arrested me. Where were the drugs he found? I thought about

Armando and wondered if he knew where I was. I thought about all the crimes I'd committed and how I was now in jail for almost nothing.

The weekend passed quickly. Jane and I sat around gossiping with the girls. Some were sick from coming off heroin. They'd occasionally run to their cell and throw up, moaning and cursing, swearing they'd stay clean when they got out. I decided that when I got out I wasn't shoplifting anymore, or hanging out with Jane.

On Monday, child advocacy lawyers came to see Jane and me. They asked us to sign papers, and then promised to have us out by morning.

Tuesday morning, we were released. Jane left an hour before me. I told her to take the bus back and I'd see her later. When it was my turn to leave, I was led through the series of locking gates, given my clothes back, and lastly, handed my purse and shoes. When they opened the final gate to release me, Zack was standing there in his denim jacket and work boots, his long hair in a single braid. He looked furious.

I walked past him, ignoring him. He chased after me, plying me with arguments on why I now had to come and live with him.

"Why, so I can end up in a detention home like Seely? Fuck you!"

"Hey, I'm still your father!"

"Your wife told lies about Seely and now she's locked up with strangers."

"Seely took money from Leona's purse, Leona wouldn't lie about that. And she ran away while I was at work, it wasn't my fault."

"You're a lousy father, and your wife is a lying bitch. Seely doesn't steal, I do." I sat down on the curb outside the jail, not sure what my next move was.

"Please, just talk to me, I'll drive you home."

I agreed and got into Zack's carpeted van. As he drove he yelled at me about how irresponsible I was, how I'd left school, and how I was going nowhere. Then, he turned onto the highway.

42

"You're going in the wrong direction."

"No, I'm taking you home with me."

"You'd better have handcuffs, and a door that locks from the outside, and never let me go to school because the second I am out of your sight, I'm gone. You can't hold me."

Zack pulled off the road and got a couple of cans of beer from the cooler in the back of his van. He handed me one. He drove me to my apartment, drinking beer the whole ride. He looked so upset I felt guilty. I had always adored my father. I grew up a daddy's girl, but this marriage, and the way he treated Seely—I just couldn't stand it.

Zack double-parked his van in front of my apartment. I jumped out. He was pretty drunk by now. He opened the window while I stood on my front porch looking for my key.

He called out, "Please change your mind, honey. I can help you."

I didn't look back at him. I used both hands to push the heavy wooden Victorian door open. I went into the hall, and then let the door go so it slammed shut hard, just like those prison gates.

Eight

Five Percenter: The Five-Percent Nation of Islam, or the Five Percenters, was founded in Harlem in 1964 by Clarence 13X. Five Percenters rename themselves. Each man views himself as a God.

Cut: An innocuous white powder that looks identical to cocaine. Cut is mixed with cocaine to increase the weight and thus the profit on a batch. Most dealers use Mannitol, an artificial sweetener sold in large brown bottles both in health food stores and head shops.

After my arrest and imprisonment, Armando took me to Las Casa, the most fancy restaurant in Southbridge. He lectured me while sipping a small glass of amber Scotch, saying that successful dealers shouldn't take drugs or be nabbed for stupid infractions like petty theft.

"Dealers should be, ah … *dignificado,* you know, always cool."

"It was Jane's fault, I didn't do anything."

"You must learn to pick better friends. Don't be *estúpida*!"

"I'm sorry, okay?" I stirred my icy daiquiri with a straw.

"Sorry is no good, no *basta*. First, you must stop tripping. No *más*. Just smoke the marijuana I gave you. It is *especial*, from God."

We laughed because God was a Five Percenter we bought pot from. He was a timid young black man with shiny Jheri curls. God had three "wives" in three apartments, and they all wore black scarves over their hair. They mostly hid in the kitchen when strangers came. He played all religious saying he was a God from outer space and complaining about "the devil's drink." But he sold heroin, ludes, pot, and hash without compunction.

The waitress came with our filet mignon and lobster tails. Armando asked her for two more drinks and a bottle of wine.

I put my hand on Armando's. "Mira, I give you my *promesa* I will quit shoplifting and taking *las drogas*."

"Chica, *su español es bueno,*" he said.

"Gracias, but I still only know a few words and I barely *comprendo*."

"Ah, but you will soon. If I take you to Colombia, you will speak perfect in one month."

The waitress returned with our drinks, and she poured our wine in glasses.

"Salud," he said, and we clinked our glasses.

Armando seemed satisfied with my promise, and we ate in silence for a while.

He broke the quiet by saying, "So, *muñeca*, will Enrique be your *amante*?"

"*Amante*? Please translate."

"I know about you and Enrique."

"*Qué*? How? Mira, I only kissed him."

"I told him never to kiss you again."

"Why would you do that?" Imagining their conversation made me feel ill.

"He's no man. I am a *caballero* and I will have you."

"What the fuck are you talking about?"

I was nervous. I wanted to ask him about Lourdes, and about the time she had two black eyes, but I was scared.

"Why do you want a boy?"

"Um, maybe because I'm a girl. Why are we having this conversation?" I still couldn't believe he knew I kissed Enrique.

"Because I want you to be my *compañera*. You know, my left-hand."

"You mean right-hand."

"Whatever you say, mi hija. We will be rich and eat here every night. But you cannot mess around with customers, especially *muchachos*. They will want to be the boss of you and I need you for my business. You are *muy inteligente* and you are *blanca*."

"Blanca … that means white?"

"Sí, who do you think is gonna buy all the coke?"

A few weeks later, Armando and I were going to the city. He was taking me with him on a coke buy. My jeans, sweater, boots—and lace gloves like Madonna's—were all black. I wore my usual heavy makeup; bright red lipstick, thick black eyeliner, and light blue sparkling eye shadow.

I heard a car honking. I looked out the window and saw Armando standing outside a dark Lincoln Town Car. I grabbed my black leather purse and jacket and ran down the stairs.

I got into my first chauffeured car. The driver gave me a glass of white wine with a cocktail napkin. During the ride, since the driver was there, Armando and I chatted idly.

Hours later we landed in the Bronx. Armando told the driver to pull over. The driver turned the car off, got out and opened our door. Then he got back in the car and started reading a newspaper.

I held Armando's arm while we walked down the sidewalk. He was carrying a leather briefcase. We passed store windows decorated with fake gold jewelry and tall colored candles bearing pictures of Christian saints.

"Who's the driver?" I asked.

"Just some car company I called."

"Why are we using a chauffer? He might see something."

"Nah, besides all I have is a briefcase. He will also love us when he gets his tip." Armando was a notorious over-tipper, and it did seem to buy him loyalty and special treatment everywhere we went.

"But what if we get pulled over?"

"Mi hija, nobody pulls over Town Cars."

We stopped at a huge redbrick apartment building. We had passed so many, it seemed to me the entire Bronx was made up of them. There had to be hundreds of apartments in each. I imagined all those different lives going on inside of one giant building.

Once we were inside the dealer's apartment, it was dark. We stood in a vestibule lit from the glow of a television in the next room. Young Latin men searched my purse and coat and even gave me a light patting down. They looked in Armando's briefcase. It was filled with money.

We were escorted through a living room full of armed men watching television. Some stood leaning against the wall, their guns hanging from straps on their shoulders, like purses. I looked at the floor, following Armando like a puppy.

Our escorts left us in a gaudy bedroom with gold drapes, a wall of mirrored closet doors, and a red chenille covered bed. I spied a machine gun standing upright in the corner.

"*Mi amigo, me alegro verte.*" A short, chubby man in his fifties shook Armando's hand jovially.

"*Sí, tú también.*"

They both looked at me and smiled. Armando introduced me to Benito. He shook my hand then gestured for Armando and me to sit on the huge bed.

Benito spoke no English. He was slovenly and wore loose fitting clothes and a beige cap over sparse hair, he was nothing like the lean, tailor dressed, well-coiffed Armando.

He went over and pulled open the mirror-covered doors. "*Cocaína! Es bueno, no es?*" It was a closet full of coke.

There were dozens of narrow shelves. On each were stacked plastic wrapped bricks, sealed with tan packing tape. I started counting and multiplying, trying to value the treasure I was looking at. I had never even seen a hundred-dollar gram of coke. Now, I was looking at more than a million dollars worth.

I thought I was the coolest girl I knew. I was a fearless, tough, daring, rule-breaking bitch. That's why I was about to leave a life of petty theft and dealing pills to become a supplier of the next big thing. I admired myself in the mirrors of the closet, my sixteen-year-old image repeated on each folding door.

Benito pulled three bricks off the shelves and tossed them on the bed next to us. They had codes written on them in black marker. He pulled out a razor blade and sliced small triangles on each, then pulled back layers of plastic wrapping. Next, he handed Armando a dollhouse sized gold spoon. Armando dug into the crystal white powder, filled the spoon, and held it out to me.

"Me? But you said I ..."

"*Tranquilo*," he said softly, "sniff this and tell me how it is."

I had never sniffed anything before. But in a movie, I saw a man snort coke through a tiny straw in one nostril while he held the other nostril closed with his thumb. So, I imitated him. The stinging powder went straight up my nose.

"*Cómo es?*" they said almost in unison.

"Good. Buena." My heart began to beat faster. This was far stronger than Rush. I started grinning and both men laughed. Armando took a spoonful from the next brick and passed it to me. What was he thinking? I had never done coke before and he was treating me like a tester. Benito asked which one we wanted. Armando looked at me sternly, so I randomly pointed to one.

Armando opened his briefcase and the men bantered for a few minutes. Benito then called a slender young man into the room. He sat down on the bed opposite me and flashed a quick, shy smile.

Handing me the briefcase Armando said, "Give Benito's boy thirty thousand dollars."

It was all twenties. I had never seen that much money before, but I'd handled plenty of cash over the past three years. And the coke-high made me feel sharp. I smoothed each bill with a tug, imitating tellers at the bank. I made piles containing a thousand dollars each.

The young man recounted my piles while Benito and Armando drank Scotch from highballs and chatted in Spanish. It takes a long time to count out thirty grand.

"Why did you make me your tester?" I asked Armando as we walked back towards the Town Car.

"I needed one. I couldn't bring anyone but you, you are my compañera."

"But I had no idea what I was picking. Plus, now I'm fucked-up."

"They're all the same."

"You don't know what you're doing."

"Ah, I know *mucho*. You will be surprised." He put his arm around me and squeezed my shoulder.

"But that was a ton of coke! And where'd you get the money?"

"It is not a ton, it is only a kilo. The dinero is mine. I made it on the pills."

"But why did you buy a kilo? That's so much, and we don't even have customers for the stuff."

I didn't like coke. It made my heart pound so hard my chest ached. There was also an acid nasal drip that burned my throat, and a nasty aftertaste in my mouth.

"The Upholders want some, and so does God," said Armando.

"You're going to sell to bikers? How do you know The Upholders?"

"I know everybody. And you are going to sell to bikers, chica. They will love you."

I didn't like bikers. The ones I met as a kid were scary racists.

On the ride home, we made a quick stop to get empanadas and once again ate the spicy beef pastries Armando so loved.

We reached Southbridge late. Armando had the driver leave us on a corner. We walked to his house, slipping in quietly because Lourdes was asleep. Armando extended his hand to me. I took it and he led me through the kitchen to a back bedroom.

Cardboard was duct taped over the window, completely covering it. There was a small bed and a coffee table. I sat on the bed. Armando left then returned with two glasses of scotch and shut the door.

"Salud! Why not roll a joint? You have not smoked all night."

He began arranging things on the table: the brick of coke, razor blades, plastic sandwich bags, a calculator, and an electronic scale the size of a dinner plate.

I lit the pot and inhaled deeply, then sipped the caramel-colored liquor.

"Chica, we are gonna make a lot of money with this stuff. *Primero*, we have to break it up."

He pulled on the tape covering the hole Hector made. He dug into the brick with his nail and offered me a pinkie finger with a tiny pile of powder on it.

"Wait, you said no more drugs just a couple of weeks ago. Do you want me hooked on coke before we even sell any?"

"No, no. If you mess with this stuff, I'll punch you right in the mouth. But tonight is *especial*. We are celebrating. *Además, hay que conocer el producto.*"

"In English, please," I said.

"Sí, sí. *Perdóneme*, I'm sorry. I said that you must know what the stuff is like to sell it."

"And you?"

He sniffed the little pile off his pinkie. Then he did it again and offered me some.

"Remember, only this once. Junkies don't make good dealers," he said.

Armando sliced through the plastic on the brick with the razor until he could pull off the casing. He carved a chunk off the block of pressed white powder and placing it on the scale, added chunks until there was an even ounce. The pieces were then scraped off the scale with a razor into a sandwich bag. Holding the bag at an angle and shaking it, he coaxed the cocaine into the corner of the baggie. He twisted the extra plastic and tied it into a tight knot then tore the excess plastic off. The coke looked as if it had been shrink-wrapped.

We cut and weighed and knotted and pulled, creating one-ounce balls of coke. Some packets only weighed 3.5 grams, an eighth of an ounce. These were called eight balls. We made them to sell to people who wanted to test the coke before buying. We threw the balls into a paper bag. Armando took a glass vial out and scraped coke into it, filling it full of powder. He handed me the vial and a velvet cloth I unrolled to find a tiny gold metal spoon and straw. Each was held with elastic, and there was an empty spot for the vial.

"It's a kit," he said. "Use it to get people high, you know, friends, people who want to try it."

Arriving home at dawn, I got into bed with my purse. The room darkening shade made it impossible to tell it was day. I turned on a bedside lamp and took out my faux makeup case. Inside were two eight balls, four ounces, and my black velvet kit. How the hell would I sell this? I put the case back in my purse, pushed it under my bed, and fell asleep.

My doorbell woke me up a few hours later. By the time I got out of bed, it was shrilling like a fire alarm; someone was holding a finger continuously on the button. I opened the window and hung my head out.

"*Pendejo*! Are you crazy?" I was sure it was one of my punk neighborhood customers jonesing for something.

"No." It was the unmistakable voice of Armando. "Chica, let me in."

I buzzed him in and raced to find clothes. I opened the door in red sweatpants and a small white tank top with a glossy strawberry ironed on.

"You look so cute, like a little girl."

"What now?"

"Now, you eat breakfast." I opened the bag he handed me and pulled out a white sugarcoated doughnut. I took bites out of it while Armando explained that we were going to meet people today.

"Take a shower, look great, and I'll be back to get you in an hour. Bring your kit and the stuff."

First place he drove me was the Lincoln Brother's. I had not seen those queens since the day I met Armando on their porch almost a year ago. I figured they were mad at me for going over their heads to their supplier.

"They're gonna hate me."

"They love you. Let's go."

I reluctantly opened the El Camino's door and got out. As we walked, my spiked heel stuck in a crack. I struggled to free myself, and Armando knelt down and pulled on my boot. I lost my balance and leaned hard on his shoulder. He looked up at me with a smile. He was so handsome, so alluring. For a moment, I thought about falling into his arms. Then, we were walking up those fated porch steps.

"*Cómo están ustedes?*" Armando smiled and heartily shook hands with Jamal and then Jaleel. "Look who I brought."

Both brothers hugged me. Jamal said, "Where you been, girl?"

"I'm sorry Jam, I know, I suck. I've just been so fucking busy."

"It's cool baby girl, but we all miss you hangin' around the place."

Jamal and me stood arm in arm. Armando asked for privacy and Jamal led us into an empty room. We all stood in a huddle.

"Mira, you have to try this shit. Pure. *Totalmente puro,*" Armando said to Jamal.

I gave sniffs to the brothers from the tiny spoon until Jaleel left the room and returned with a razor blade and mirror. I dumped some coke on the mirror and he formed the powder into lines with the razor. They sniffed them with the straw.

"Man, that is some good shit. Serious," Jamal said.

"Do you want some?" Armando asked.

"How much?"

"Fifteen-hundred. It is totally pure, uncut. You can add cut and still get a hundred a gram. You pay her. And when you want more, you call her."

Jamal left and returned with the cash. I handed him one of the ounces.

"Thanks babygirl." He kissed me full on the lips as always. I was so relieved we were cool; I really loved Jamal. I had spent many hours at this house smoking pot and watching The Little Rascals while waiting for my order.

"She's working for me now, so careful." Armando poked a finger playfully in Jamal's chest.

"I see, yes, I see." Jamal grinned.

"You don't see nothing, bitch." I gave Jamal a slight shove. Armando asked to use a phone, and we all followed him back toward the kitchen.

"So, he's your man now? What happened to that cute blonde white boy you brought sometimes, the one with those tight jeans?"

"That was, like, two years ago. He's history … and Armando's not my man."

"Okay girlfriend. Whatever you say."

We laughed. Jamal slapped my ass affectionately.

Armando finished his call and we said our goodbyes. Jamal hugged me tightly.

"Come over anytime, baby. And I'll definitely call you," he said.

Armando and I returned to his car just as dusk hit.

"Muchacha, we just made almost six-hundred dollars!"

We were both excited. Maybe this cocaine thing would work out after all.

We drove across town to *gringo* land, where The Upholders were housed in a degenerate Victorian. A rusty iron fence lined the garbage filled yard. We tiptoed past the broken beer bottles and empty motor oil cans. I held onto Armando. We entered the kitchen and Armando introduced me to Quinn, the leader.

"Is this your wife?" Quinn asked Armando.

"No, she works for me."

"Have a chair, little girl." I smiled and sat down next to a fish tank where toothy piranhas swam. There were a few hookers hanging about. We gave a friendly nod to each other. "Chicks, get lost," said Quinn, and the girls wandered into the adjacent living room.

Armando, still standing, told Quinn about the coke. I pulled the kit out of my bag, unrolling the black velvet with trembling hands, and removed the vial. Quinn swiped it out of my hand.

"Gimme the spoon, girl, come on," he said, holding out his hand.

I gave him the spoon and looked around while he took snorts. I'd never been to a biker den, but I had read a really scary book about Hells Angels.

The walls were plastered with stickers of skull and crossbones. Confederate flags hung here and there. It was dark. The windows were completely boarded over. The kitchen opened to a large room where bikers sprawled on dirty couches while watching porn. They wore white T-shirts, faded jeans, and leather vests with patches.

Quinn smirked and slammed a hand down on the table. "Gimme an ounce, little girl!"

I pulled an ounce out and tossed it on the table.

"How much?"

"Fifteen."

"Expensive."

"It is the best, my friend, straight from Colombia with no cut," said Armando. "If you like it I have a steady supply. You will deal with her."

"I deal with the girlie? Is that right?"

"Mira, uh ... look, she is my girlfriend, *comprendo?*"

"Yeah, that's cool, man." He pulled out a roll of bills in an elastic band and dropped it on the table. "Here, girlfriend, I'll take two."

I tossed another ounce on the table then quickly counted the money and put it in my purse.

"Here's my number." I handed him a notebook page with my phone number written on it. Quinn ripped open the ounce and shined a flashlight on it. "This looks amazing, lots of crystal. I'll call ya."

"You're a fucking cabrón!" I yelled at Armando on the ride home. "And you drive like shit. Chill out, so we don't get pulled over."

"Come on, muchacha, I'll take you to dinner."

"Fuck your dinner. Those bikers are assholes. You're going to get me raped."

"That's why I said you were my girlfriend."

"Yeah, that'll help."

"They respect business. They won't hurt you because they will want a lot more of that coke. They're gonna need us. Come on, *chiquita*, we just made over a thousand."

We went to dinner at La Casa to celebrate.

I got home around midnight. I sat at the kitchen table chain smoking Marlboros. Bikers always made me think of my father. He always rode me around on his motorcycle, even when I was so small I had to sit in front of him so he could hold me onto the seat. I decided to call him at work the next day and asked him to come to dinner.

When my father arrived, I gave him a bowl of homemade chili. We didn't talk about our fight last month or the fact we'd barely spoke in almost a year.

"Just so you know, sweetie, you can always come home with me," he said.

"Just stop. I'm never, ever, coming to your hell house."

"Well, I'll visit again soon, if that's okay?"

"Yeah, daddy, definitely. Listen, before you go, do you want to try some coke?"

I laid lines out on my kitchen table with a razor and handed him the straw.

My father's face remained solemn. He simply took the metal straw from me, his slanted eyes oblique.

"You're selling this now?" He snorted the line, "how much?"

Nine

Peter, in a black chauffeur's uniform and cap, picked me up at my apartment in a stretch limo. I felt like a queen. I gave no thought to the fact I was leaving a Latino ghetto in a limo, and that my neighbors spent an inordinate amount of time looking out their windows.

I studied my neighborhood from behind tinted glass. Then, the limo eased onto the highway. Past rolling hills and craggy trees, I could see the river glimmering. I was becoming accustomed to rides in a chauffeured car. Sometimes I read, since I always had a Penguin Classic stashed in my large purse. Or I worked on my business books; elaborate accounting written in cryptic code. And I always drank white wine.

Last month Armando told me he had a potential new Miami connection.

"How do you know people in Miami?" I asked. I was incredulous.

"Qué?" He looked off into the distance and I took a sip of my Daiquiri. We were having dinner at La Casa. As Armando predicted, it had become a haunt.

I tried again. "So, you're going to Miami?"

"Sí. Tell no one."

"I would never."

Now, I was picking him up from the airport, excited to hear what happened in Miami.

"Chica! *Cómo estás?*" Armando handed his large leather suitcase to Peter and clasping my shoulders kissed each cheek. "Another *victoria!*" He plucked the gold St. Christopher medallion from among the hairs on his chest and kissed it.

"Peter, put my case inside the car," he said.

Peter, a tall man around twenty-five with an earnest face, did as requested. He stood at attention waiting for us to climb into the limo. As we were getting in, Armando handed him a crumpled hundred-dollar bill.

"Isn't that excessive? This whole ride only costs three-hundred," I said.

"Excessive is how we must be. We are working, here, in this car."

"But we're not holding, are we?"

"Chica, we are *transportando.*"

"And the driver knows?"

"He knows *nada.*"

Armando opened his suitcase. He rifled through silk shirts and linen pants to pull out a gift-wrapped shirt box. He unwrapped it and showed me the brick, not much smaller than the box. "Twenty-thousand, chica, twenty! Ten-thousand less than the Bronx. We will see how the people like it, *te parece bien.*"

"But the plane, is it cool?"

"*Muy* cool. I went right through the x-ray with this. You'll see."

"Me?"

"*Sí. Usted. Usted vendrá conmigo a la Florida.*"

"What? You know I don't speak Spanish."

"Ah, but you will soon. It is the only language. I said that you will come with me to Florida."

Sometimes I thought Armando was a racist, especially when he talked so proudly of being a true "Spaniard" and he called Puerto Ricans "perros," meaning "dogs," and white people "gringos." I was never interested in nationalism, and I thought racists were stupid and mean. And the only imperialism I was truly interested in was my own.

Still, I learned a fair bit of Spanish. Armando made almost every sentence a quick Spanish lesson. Understanding Spanish was a desire of mine for only one reason, though: I wanted to know everything Armando said. During deals, while he talked on the phone, or when he spoke to Lourdes, I sat silently listening to the slippery vowels of rapid Spanish, having little idea what was being said.

Armando was dubious. Sometimes he slipped out of view for days into worlds I knew nothing about. Listening attentively to his numerous phone booth calls was futile. They were always in Spanish. As far as I could tell, I was the only *gringa* he knew. Questions were forbidden, but I asked them anyway. Armando usually replied with chilly silence or a warning glance. When I did receive answers, the replies were suspect. I knew nothing about huge portions of his life. Where he had spent his twenties, if he was married before, how he met Lourdes, everything he'd done between when he jumped off that naval ship in Florida at age twenty, and when I met him on the Lincoln's porch at age thirty-five, was a black hole.

Pouring scotch for Armando now, as the stretch limo took us home, we were celebrating his smuggling and negotiating victory. With determination and will, he was creating a cocaine business. Impressed and intimidated, I sat on a low seat next to the bar and handed him his drink. I poured myself a glass of wine.

"*Aquí, vea la cocaína.*" Pulling back clear packing tape, he revealed a small, razor-cut hole shimmering with white, crystal powder. Offering me a taste on my tongue, he told me this is how we will now test our bricks upon receipt. It burned and then numbed my mouth, exactly as it was supposed to.

"This Miami cocaine is better, it is only cheaper because I took risk smuggling it on the plane."

"So this is going to be a regular thing now?"

"Sí. I bought a house on Key Biscayne. *Es pequeña*, but *elegante.* You will see it soon."

"Wait, what? How did you buy a house?"

"Chica, I told you I have many amigos. You will meet them, they are very good people, they are from my country." He smiled peacefully, maintaining an air of contentment.

My mind raced with questions, none of which I asked.

"Chica let us go to the city to celebrate. Tell Peter to take us to Manhattan."

I pushed a button that unrolled the dark glass between the driver and us and asked him to stop in Manhattan.

"My pleasure," he replied, "the address?"

"Fifty-one and Eight Avenue," Armando replied.

"Eighth," I corrected.

"Eighth. Sí. *Octavo.*"

A short time later, we arrived at *Asadera Carbena.*

"Colombian food, chica, *la mejor comida del mundo!*"

"Qué?"

He kissed my cheek, "the best food in the world!"

"What about the cocaína?"

He had taped it closed again and wrapped it in a shirt. Placing it in his briefcase he declared, "I'm a businessman."

Peter parked the limo. He hopped out of the driver's seat and walked to the back of the long car, opening the door for us in a courtly manor. We emerged from our miniature room on wheels and went straight into the restaurant. The men greeted Armando heartily. He smiled big and shook hands with them cheerfully.

"You know them?"

"Sí. I know everybody, chica. Let us celebrate." His broad grin was gorgeous.

"Why are you so happy?"

"Happy? Chica, *tengo todo*! Means, um ... I have all."

We got drunk at dinner. Armando ordered bottles of champagne and all the food, since the menu was in Spanish. Sweet plantains, rice with coconut and *Biste a Caballo*, a spicy beef dish, covered the table. After we finished eating, he stood up. Without a word, he came to my side of the table, sliding into the booth with me.

"What are you doing?" I looked around the room. All the wait staff seemed to be watching us and smiling. "Come on, what's up?"

I was draped in his cologne. He took my face firmly in both hands and kissed me. At first, I thought it might be some kind of special Colombian thank you kiss. Then he kissed me more, and with his tongue.

"What are you doing?" I tried to squirm free from his grasp.

"Celebrating, chica, come're."

I had no idea he liked me that way. Before I could think, he kissed me again and I softened, sliding my arms under his coat to hold him closer. I thought of Lourdes and José and money and white powder. Then, my mind went blank, the world disappeared, and I fell into that kiss. After a few minutes Armando stopped, offering me his hand. "*Ven*, come, come."

He grabbed the champagne bottle off the table, hastily paid the bill, and pulled me out of the restaurant. The limo was steps away, but we passed a small shop, and I exclaimed, "Snoopy!" eyeing a large stuffed animal in the window. Armando walked towards the store, pulling me along as I protested.

"The Snoopy doll," he said to the counter clerk, who pulled it from the display window.

"That'll be sixty-dollars."

"Sixty-dollars! Is it stuffed with gold?" He snorted, throwing a hundred-dollar bill on the counter. Placing the stuffed animal in my arms he said, "*Aquí amor.*"

I knew enough Spanish to know what he said. Embarrassed, I looked down at the floor, holding Snoopy tight.

We walked toward the limo. Armando, a smartly dressed middle-aged man with a long wool coat, polish shined shoes, dressy black slacks secured with a narrow belt, and a gray silk shirt. He was holding a briefcase in his right hand and an open bottle of Champagne in his left. And trailing a few steps behind, me, a slight sixteen-year-old girl with glittery eye makeup, wearing a black leather jacket with brightly stitched Jordache jeans, teetering on heels, clutching a huge stuffed Snoopy.

PART TWO

PART TWO

Ten

Drop: When a drug supplier delivers a preordered amount of drugs to a drug dealer.

Ki: Short for Kilo. Pronounced like the word "key."

Armando pressed the button on the console between us and spoke to the chauffer through the half-open interior window.

"You can leave us *aquí*, uh, here."

"Why here?" I felt jumpy. It was past midnight and we were five blocks south of Armando's apartment with a kilo of coke.

He glared at me as we got out of the car, which was my reminder not to ask questions. Unspeaking, we walked down the icy sidewalk past rows of seemingly endless attached brick row houses.

Having spent the past two hours making out with Armando in the limo, I decided he was one of the best kissers I'd met. But when he pawed at my top or his hands wandered to the button of my jeans I pushed him away, sometimes moving to the seat across from him. He was married and we were business partners. Having an affair with him seemed imprudent to the point of reckless.

It was easy to push him away in the limo. There was no way for me to relax with the driver only inches away. Despite the tinted window separating us, I was sure Peter knew we were messing around.

Armando stopped abruptly and pulled out his keys.

"What are you doing?"

"This is my new house."

"House? You have a house in Southbridge now too?"

"Sí."

"Is Lourdes here?"

"No."

"Where is she?"

"Florida," he turned keys in brass locks until the front door opened. Holding his hand out he gestured for me to go in ahead of him. The room was dark. We stood in the shadows.

"What about your apartment? Why is Lourdes in Florida?"

"Tranquilo, shh, *mi amor*." Taking my hand, he pulled me towards wooden stairs that hugged the wall to our right. Walking up them, I ran my free hand over the pocked plaster. My other hand remained tightly in Armando's grip.

We went into Armando's bedroom, locking the door though we were alone in the house. The shades were tightly drawn. I lingered near the window, peeking under the shade to view the small backyard. Armando went to a hexagonal wooden end table and turned on a small white lamp. Next, he opened the closet door and dug through a large pile of clothes to find a gray metal box with a handle and large combination lock square in the center.

"Mira, look."

It was a six hundred pound safe that four deliverymen had carried up the stairs. He told me the salesman assured him that it was fireproof. He unlocked it and inside was a small chamber with a horizontal shelf. The bottom was stacked with neat piles of cash. He placed the kilo, still in the gift-wrapped shirt box, on the shelf. Closing the safe door, he mindlessly spun the lock.

"We'll cut it up tomorrow, mi hija. Come be with me."

"No, I can't. I gotta go."

"But I need you." He took my hand and pulled me towards the bed. "Let me show you what it is like to be with a real man, a caballero."

Wrestling me down on the bed, he began to kiss me.

"Cabrón! *Estúpido!* Let go!"

I stood up and walked across the bedroom. Sitting down on a velvety gray stuffed chair, I rolled a joint. Armando sat on the edge of the bed watching me.

"What about Lourdes?"

"She is okay. I told her you will be my girlfriend."

"Why the fuck would you do that?"

"*Muñeca*, I am a man, from Colombia. It is my *cultura.*"

"You never even kissed me before tonight. I thought we were *compañeros.*"

"I have been wanting all this time to be with you. Didn't you know?"

I really didn't know, but I had thought about kissing him sometimes. Especially when his thick accent made the plainest word sound exquisite.

I lit the joint and took a deep inhale. Armando reached his hand out and I brought him the joint. Occasionally, he'd take a single puff.

"You will stay with me." He grabbed my wrist. "I'm a man, not one of your boys! You cannot tease me like this."

I gave in.

Under the covers, he pulled me into his arms and whispered a great many things, all in Spanish. There was little foreplay. Armando made love to me clumsily. He was not adept like the other men I'd known. Still, he was sweet and puppyish.

Conflicting thoughts and feelings rushed through me; fear, excitement, dread, panic, and the delicious high of committing yet another forbidden act.

"*Negrita*, caress me." He spoke softly, and nuzzled under my neck.

"What does that mean?"

"Negrita. It means … um … my girl. Now, caress me."

I had never caressed a man before and it seemed strange. Men had caressed me but that was before, not after, sex. He fell asleep. I got up from bed and found the joint. I was excited at the prospect of being Armando's girlfriend, but I was also worried about things. I wondered if Lourdes really knew and if she minded. And what about that time she had two black eyes?

I lit my joint and sat in the dark smoking and calculating how much profit I would make tomorrow, when I made my drops.

In the morning, Armando woke me up kissing my neck.

"I think I'm hung over." I rubbed my head.

"I'll get you breakfast. You'll feel *mucho mejor*."

"No, we need to cut the ki up. I gotta get to work."

He dressed and ran down the steps. I heard the front door slam and I jumped out of bed. I surveyed the house looking in closets, cabinets, and bathrooms for signs of Lourdes. There were none. Like the apartment, this house had not one decoration and almost no furniture. The living room set, a gray velour sectional straight out of the seventies, faced a large TV on a dark wood cabinet. On the windowsill, the requisite

Saint's candle burned in a tall jar. This one with a picture of the Virgin Mary pasted onto the glass.

Armando came back with spicy tamales and coffee. We ate at the simple round kitchen table on blue flower trimmed Correll. By now, I was sure this whole house had been furnished from the Salvation Army store, probably in one day.

It was past noon and I had to get home to shower and change. I told Armando to start packaging and I'd be back in an hour. Walking the five blocks home gave me time alone to freak out in my head. My apartment seemed unfamiliar. I took a long shower, leaning against the pink tiles and sobbing in tiny bursts.

I downed a glass of vodka from the frosty bottle I kept in the freezer while I dressed up for my deliveries. Driving back to Armando's, I fretted over how to now act around him. When I arrived at his door, he kissed me and pulled me inside. He had finished packaging what I needed. I sat on his bed placing ounces of coke in a zippered black case and writing records in my book. He glanced over the accounts nodding in agreement and pushed me down on the bed.

"I gotta go to work." I pushed him away and stood up.

"Sí. After, we will have dinner."

"I'll call you later." I tossed the case in my purse, hurrying down the stairs and outside, into the late afternoon light. It was time to make my deliveries.

In the past six weeks, I'd sold the entire kilo Armando had bought in the Bronx. We cut it up with razors and packaged it into ounces. I delivered it as requested to our three customers. Now, I will sell them the Miami cocaine Armando says is better.

Getting into the Nova, I began psyching myself up to start my rounds. Whenever I went out selling (or buying) there was always a flutter of nerves reminding me that tonight my bed might be a cot in a jail cell. I pushed the scary thoughts away, using mind control methods I'd read in the Seth books. I focused instead on imagining the piles of money that would cover my bed at home that night.

Eleven

February 1985

Age 16

A Bump: a small dose of a drug, usually heroin or cocaine.

Visiting the Upholders' clubhouse weekly the past few months had made me less afraid of them. Each time I left intact, my confidence grew. The bikers hanging around me were lug heads that loyally followed the orders of their pack leader, Quinn, who was clearly the smartest among them. I counted on him to protect me, though he had a malevolent streak that often reminded me I was dealing with a rogue.

Sitting at the dirty kitchen table among overflowing ashtrays, trying not to touch anything, I pulled my black case and small notebook out of my purse.

"What do you need?" I smiled warmly in order to hide my contempt.

"I'll take six."

"Six. Okay, that'll be nine-thousand."

A small thud sounded as he tossed the elastic bound pile of money on the table. I counted it briskly. Quinn had bought every ounce I had on me. The amount our customers were buying was rapidly increasing. I would need to go back to Armando's to replenish my stock.

As I was counting the bills, Quinn asked me about being with Armando. "Why you wanna be with a nigger?"

"Excuse me?"

"Ya know, you're a pretty girl. You don't need to degrade yourself."

Armando was rather dark-skinned, but I had never thought about it.

"I might be mixed myself. My mother's father," I said, lying.

Quinn laughed and took a long drink off of a brown Budweiser bottle. "You're a white girl. That's bullshit."

"Well, no one knows for sure, because my grandmother never married. She had a baby by herself." I switched the true story of my great-grandmother with my grandmother's, to make it sound like I contained even more of the questionable blood. My great-grandmother's lover was actually Irish.

Quinn ran his fingers through thick curls. His chunky arms were covered in stretchy tattoos and his shirtless belly hung low over a brass Harley Davidson belt buckle. "Hey, no disrespect girlfriend, seriously." He held a meaty hand out to me and I shook it, not making eye contact with him.

I had lied to Quinn hoping he would stop making racist remarks. I also wanted to repulse him. He was flirtatious with me and I responded coquettishly. It was a part of the job I usually enjoyed, but with Quinn it made me sick. As I stood to leave, Quinn spoke without looking up from the lines of coke he was cutting up on a mirror.

"Girlfriend, you're definitely a white bitch. I know, because I'd fuck ya."

I walked out and casually called over my shoulder, "Very funny." Another part of my job is not to tell the customer they are an asshole, especially when they are.

Knocking on the door at Armando's minutes later was the first time I'd ever come to his house without phoning first. Opening the door just a crack, he looked surprised to see me.

"Negrita, you just left."

"Well, I'm sold out. Can you let me in?"

In the living room there were two young girls on the sofa. One had a baby in her arms.

"This is Jill and Coco," he said, meekly introducing them. I glared at him, then smiled and said hello to the girls.

They looked at each other nervously and each said a soft, "*Como esta?*"

I looked at Armando with narrowed eyes. "Can I talk to you, please?"

"Sí," he answered, walking towards the kitchen.

I followed him. "I want them out of here."

"They're just kids, negrita."

"Well I have fucking work to do. Make them leave, now, cabrón!"

I watched from the kitchen while he spoke rapid Spanish to them. He handed one of them a small piece of tinfoil. One was a freckled blonde, the other clearly Hispanic, with a long black ponytail and light-brown skin. Definitely hookers, they were no more than fourteen.

After they left, I stomped up the stairs to Armando's bedroom and threw my bag onto his bed. Pulling out my book, moneybag, and black pouch, I sat on the bed while Armando opened the safe.

"Count this, chulo." I tossed the money at him.

"Negrita, I gave them a few lines. Qué?"

"They're hookers."

"Sí."

"Fuck, just gimme six more ounces, the scummy bikers cleaned me out."

"That is good. *Aquí*, mi amor," he said while handing me more ounces.

I fumed in silence while he counted the money I gave him. I shrank from his touch when he tried to embrace me.

"Get off me. You already want me to share you with your wife."

"Sí. It is okay in my country."

"Fuck you and your stupid country."

"I swear, muñeca, I would never fuck them. On my *San Cristóbal*." He touched the gold medallion around his neck.

"I gotta go."

"I'll see you for dinner?"

Ignoring him, I trotted down the stairs and out the front door, focusing on my deliveries. People were waiting for me. No thoughts of Armando were allowed to enter my head as I finished making my rounds. I couldn't afford to have them break my concentration. This had been the most financially lucrative day of my life and I wanted to be happy.

I drove two blocks to God's house. He welcomed me, and offered me a cold can of ginger ale. I took it and sat down at the long wooden table in his living room.

"Hey, God, why is your name God?" His eccentricity had fascinated me since we first met.

He passed me a tract while he sat weighing the ounces I had put on the table. The tract said white people were the devil, and five percent of men were gods from outer space. It was full of racist "facts" so bizarre that I found it funny. God was soft-spoken and not very bright. He smiled often with the mischievous grin of a little boy. He didn't possess the heart of a racist.

I looked up from reading the tract and he was smiling.

"I'm white, am I a devil?"

"Yes you are. You're a devil woman."

"You're crazy."

"Seriously, you make me want to be bad … real bad." Giggling, he covered his smile with his hand.

"And your three wives?"

"A man can dream." He winked at me while passing me a pile of cash. "Please don't tell your man. I'm just playin'"

"What man?"

"Armando. He says you're his girl."

I leaned across the table and kissed his cheek. "It'll be our secret." His ebony skin revealed nothing but I'm sure he blushed. God was a poser. He wasn't racist, or even religious. Multiple "wives" was as radical as he got. He housed and supported each woman, and spent time with them and his kids. That was more than some men I knew did, and they only had one woman.

Driving three blocks to the Lincoln brothers was my final call that day. I couldn't wait to get there. While I hugged Jamal tightly, he cooed, "Babygirl, what's up? Here come sit with me." He sat down on a kitchen chair and pulled me down until I was in his lap. He hugged me hard with strong arms and I relaxed into the smell of coconut, incense, and Afro Sheen.

"Come on now, tell Jamal what's wrong."

Running my fingers along his cornrows, I avoided his question.

"Girl, that feels good, mmm. Now listen, I got a John waiting in my boudoir. Can you hang out ten minutes? I'll give you a bump."

"Bitch, when have I ever taken a bump? Gimme some hash."

Laughing, he passed me some hash and a small metal pipe. "Ten minutes, girlfriend, I promise."

I smoked the hash sitting on a small couch in a dim room where a crowd of junkies watched TV. Jaleel and Javon both sat next to me. I passed them the pipe. Jaleel asked me if I brought their order. I said I did, but I was waiting for Jamal. He nodded slowly. The two of them sat quietly, neither having the zest of their elder brother.

An older black man who was wearing a tan suit came in. He tapped Javon's shoulder. Whispering ensued. Javon got up, disappearing with the man behind hanging strands of brightly colored plastic beads.

Jaleel remained with me. He had slow-moving liquid eyes that made me think he was gentle. Later, I learned those eyes were made slow by smoking too much angel dust.

Jamal emerged twenty minutes later, taking my hand and leading me through the curtain of beads with Jaleel following close behind. We went to Jamal's bedroom.

"Sit here, babygirl, and tell me all about it." He turned to his younger brother, "Leel, she's having some problems with her chulo." Jamal lit a rock in a clear glass pipe and passed it to me. I took a drag, inhaling the sharp burn of freebase, knowing Armando would freak if he found out I had smoked coke.

"I have no chulo, you're the one givin' all your dollars to your daddy," I said.

"Hssss! Now who's kickin' it?"

"Come on, you know Armando's not my pimp."

"Yeah girl, stick with that." Jamal sucked at his teeth, making a sound of disapproval.

Jaleel choked back a laugh, managing to hold in the large drag of coke he just inhaled.

"Let's just make the deal, Jamal. I gotta go." I was disappointed, but it was my own fault. Why did I think a coked-up queen had any advice for me?

I took an ounce out and tossed it on the bed.

"We'll take two, baby." Jamal started taking the cash out of his pocket as I completed my record day.

Jamal took my hand in his. "Now listen up girl, I don't know what's all up with you, but don't let any pricks take advantage of you. You all that, we always say you're our favorite white girl." We all giggled and passed the pipe around again.

He continued, "You know I love you. Since the day I met you at the liquor store, when you were a little girl looking for acid, and I took you home. All my brothers love you too. Don't let no bitches rob you. Don't let them fuck you up."

"Yeah, I won't, it's cool." I said.

Jamal walked holding hands with me to my car. He gave me a kiss then snapped my bra strap under my coat. I kicked him in the shin, and he feigned limping up the porch steps to his house.

I drove the Nova six blocks to my apartment, parallel parking on my narrow one-way street. Jamal, God and Quinn all thought I was Armando's girlfriend. He had now officially placed me under his protection, since girlfriends were property. But I still felt afraid.

It was deep, nagging fear I pushed away with drinking, sex, and the adrenaline thrill of making piles of money.

At my apartment, I grabbed vodka from the freezer and went into my bedroom. I closed the door, preparing to sit on my bed and do my accounting for the day. The coke smoking had given me a headache, though, so I sat back and hit the vodka straight from the bottle. I fell asleep for a few hours, until the phone by my bed was ringing continuously, like an alarm clock.

"What?" I yelled into the phone, because I knew who it was.

"Negrita, thank god. I'm coming over."

I fell back asleep until the doorbell dragged me from bed.

"Mira, we must talk about us."

"Look, *maricón*, I'm fucking sleeping."

"Just say you'll come to dinner. And we should do books first, at *mi casa*."

"*Bien*. I'll be there tomorrow. Just get rid of your whores before I come."

"*No me hables así*! Do not speak like that to me. Do not disrespect me."

"Alright, alright, would you just fucking leave already?"

He wouldn't leave. He picked me up, carrying me to my bed. He took off all of my clothes. "Just let me kiss you, *buenas noches*."

I let him. Much later that night he slipped out, leaving me warm in my bed and too tired to think about anything.

The next evening I stood knocking at Armando's door, my feet ice cold in shiny red pumps.

"Negrita, *ven*, come," he kissed my lips lightly and took my hand. "We are not going out. Me, I cooked."

"Qué? You cook?"

"Sí."

"What are we having?"

"Habas y arroz."

"Let's see … something and rice … wait … rice and beans?"

"Sí. But not like the *basura* here. This is not Puerto Rican rice. It is true Spanish beans and rice."

"Can we eat after the books? I want to get paid."

We went to Armando's bedroom. I took out my accounting book and opened my zippered bank bag, dropping the piles of money I'd collected onto his bed. We counted and stacked it. Then we reviewed the notes in my book together, and agreed on numbers. I then tore the page out of the book, and shredded it into confetti.

He tossed my cut, a pile of bills in a rubber band, across the bed. There was no discussion about how much I should get, or what the net profit was. Armando was the owner of this enterprise. But when I counted my pile and it contained fifteen hundred dollars, all I cared about is how I was gonna spend it. I've been craving a gold ring, and maybe a necklace. In one evening, I had made the amount of money I used to make in two months. I felt rich. I felt like no one could touch me or harm me. I felt invincible.

We ate the rice and beans with a bottle of red wine. I studied the pattern of the tiny floral trim on my plate in silence. The only person I knew with these dishes was my grandmother.

"Negrita, you must tell me."

"I found you with hookers. *Por que*? You already have a wife, and you made me your mistress."

"What is this word, mistress?" As I explained the usual scenario he protested. "No, we are not like that. Lourdes knows of us and I will be only yours and hers. You are like … *una pequeña* wife. *Comprendes*?"

"Una pequeña … that means small?"

"Sí, sí, small wife."

"And the hookers?"

"I won't have sex with them. Only, you know, like a BJ."

"Did you just say blowjob?"

"Sí. Por qué?"

"No, I don't want you to!" I started to cry. "And what about me, can I get a BJ on the side?"

"You do and I will punch you right in the fucking mouth." He shook his fist at me.

"Why can't me and Lourdes be enough? Why?"

"*Por qué tú me estás haciendo loco?* It is just a blowjob, I am not going to fuck them!" Tossing his napkin on the table in disgust he got up and launched into a torrent of Spanish.

He went into the unlit living room. Sitting on the sofa he took a deep sigh. "Negrita, come here."

I went and sat beside him. He took my left hand and studied it, turning it over in his hands. "Me, I love you. I moved Lourdes and José to Florida. We have business there now. And I can spend half the week with them there, and half here with you. Don't you love me?"

I didn't answer. We sat silent for a long time in the dark room. The candle flame that made the Virgin Mary glow dropped lower and lower towards the bottom of the tall jar, until liquid wax extinguished the flame.

Twelve

Turn on: Slang for getting someone high.

Sometimes I was lonely. On weekdays, my friends spent the days in school and the evenings at home with their parents. Chrissy came to see me often last summer, but now I never saw her. Her boyfriend didn't approve of me and our lifestyles could not have been more different.

Seely now lived nearby, in a row house in Spanish Town, but she was busy with her boyfriend and his family. She ran away from the detention home in February to live with Mike. He had gotten his mother, Alice, to agree that Seely could live there. Alice was a kind and generous lady. She treated Seely like a daughter, enrolling her in school and giving her a curfew. Alice and Seely grocery shopped, cooked, and cleaned house together.

My married boyfriend was out of town half the week getting us more drugs to sell and spending time with his family. I generally spent afternoons at Hector's, where everybody knew my name, but nobody spoke English. I drank daiquiris while exchanging smiles with male patrons who occasionally got up and came towards me. The bartender, in hurried Spanish, swiftly warded them off.

I'm sure he said something like, "Watch out, that's a gangster's moll!"

A girl with pixie cut red hair, an impish smile, and flashing eyes interrupted the monotony one afternoon.

"Hey, you want some company?" Before I could answer, she tossed her purse on the bar and jumped onto the stool next to me. "Not too many of us gringas around here, right? I'm Colleen."

I smiled at her panache.

She ordered a glass of white wine, but within an hour we were downing shots of Schnapps and laughing like schoolgirls who had been friends for years.

"So who keeps you?" she asked me in a hushed tone.

"Oh, you know, some guy," I said, lying.

"Mine's a pilot. He's away a lot. I get lonely."

"How old are you?"

"Seventeen," she said sighing, as if she already felt old.

"I'm sixteen," I said.

"Yeah, girlfriend? You look so much older."

"Really? Thanks, you too!"

"My mother moved to Chicago with her new husband and I never knew my father." She looked off in the distance while absently playing with a stirrer. "It's not like I'm a hooker, it's just one guy. Well, actually, there were two before him, but I've been on my own since fourteen. Estéban is thirty-eight and he's rich. He owns a townhouse."

"My mother left for a new husband, too. She lives pretty close, but I can't live there. He's a scumbag."

"And your man?" Colleen placed a hand on my arm. She was strangely serene and affectionate.

84

"He's sweet. He's away on business … hey, if you're interested, I've got some blow on me."

"No shit, girlfriend! Let's go to the ladies room."

Colleen sat on the edge of a dirty sink. The fluorescent light gave her a sallow complexion. I cut up lines on my compact mirror while I leaned against the door. We took turns snorting lines, and then I gave her a few more lines while I passed.

"Don't you like coke?" she asked.

"Not really, it makes my heart beat so fast. Plus my man … he'd kill me."

"It makes me really horny."

We laughed and I put my kit away.

"Let's go for dinner, chica, I know a great Mexican place," Colleen said.

"I'm too fucked up to drive."

"It's a little dive a few blocks away, we'll walk."

"Oh, you mean *El Conditas*."

"Sí, I do."

We went outside in the chilly early evening. I shoved my hands deep in my pockets, steeling myself against the sharp wind. Colleen held my arm, nuzzling up to me while we walked.

We quickly became best friends. We had breakfast most days at lunchtime in a greasy spoon on Main Street. We spent the afternoons in bars and went to dinner in the evenings. We shopped together, and I insisted on buying her presents of clothes and shoes. I thought about her so much, I questioned my sanity. Once, I bought her a giant white stuffed bear. I'm sure Colleen eventually figured out that my man was a dealer, but she didn't ask questions and I spoke little about him.

We disappeared for days on each other when our men came to town. It was understood. I thought of her going to dinners and movies, and sleeping with her boyfriend. But I was sure she did not imagine me driving around to the houses of bikers, Five Percenters, and male hookers, raking in thousands selling the coke Armando brought back on the plane from Miami. I went out to dinner also, though with a man who sometimes got the waitresses' phone number while I was in the bathroom, and who called his wife from my apartment each night before bed to say goodnight and talk about his son in Spanish, while I rolled and smoked my endless joints.

There was also the sex that got better with time, but never fulfilled me. I wished I were free to date without the threat of beatings over my head. I didn't really think Armando would hit me but I was afraid of what he might actually do, which I sensed might be worse.

He was jealous and possessive. Once while we were in bed he said, "Chica, you fuck like a *puta*. Porque? Why?"

"Because all the girls I know are hookers. They tell me things to do."

"Oh," he said. He turned away, his eyes looking thoughtfully into space. I waited, holding my breath. I was terrified he'd ask me questions about the guys before him. He didn't think I was a virgin, but he knew nothing of my exploits with men.

"You never got money for it, right?" he said.

"No!"

"Good. I like my *mujer* to be clean. You are mine now, right, only with me?"

"Of course," I said.

"Do you swear, on the gold cross you wear?"

I lifted the cross off my bare chest and held it tight in my fingers, "I swear, Armando, I swear to you."

He lay back, pulling me to his hairy chest and holding me tightly. "Good, because I love you. You are my everything, *mi amore.*"

There was vulnerability in his questions. He sounded young and needy. I suddenly realized how insecure and clingy he was.

And I was a liar who would swear lies on a cross, or on a bible, or on my Mother's life.

I gushed to Armando about Colleen for weeks until he said, "Why not invite her out for a drink with us? I want to meet your friend."

So I did. We planned to meet at Hector's one night after Armando and I had dinner. He now drove a brand-new shiny-black Camaro, and he sped through the narrow streets of Southbridge even faster than before.

"Cabrón, estúpido, slow down … you're gonna kill us!" I yelled at Armando as he drove. He ran a red light and I punched him in the arm.

"Mother-fucker, stop it!"

He just laughed. He enjoyed making me furious.

"You're going to kill us, Armando. Or kill someone. You're gonna crash this new car like you did the El Camino."

"That was nothing. It wasn't my fault."

"I predicted it so many times," I said.

"Well, you maybe gave me bad luck."

"Vete para carajo! You drive like a pendejo. Why won't you just slow the fuck down?"

"I told you, nothing will ever happen to you. I am your protection.

We drove on and I prayed in my head, reciting psalm ninety-one. I had memorized it. It was sometimes called the prayer for protection.

Armando and I walked into Hector's, tipsy from the drinks we had at dinner. Colleen was already sitting at the bar. I introduced them and Armando quickly sat between us on a barstool. Armando passed me change to keep the jukebox playing. Hours went by with Armando taking turns talking to us. I often couldn't hear Colleen and him over the music. He seemed charmed by her. He bought us all shots of peach Schnapps. Armando told me to turn Colleen on in the bathroom, giving me a piece of foil with a chunk of blow in it.

"Negrita, not for you."

"Why not, you want her to have fun and not me?"

"Chica, you work. She's a puta, she can get hooked and it doesn't matter. Just do what I say."

Colleen and I staggered to the bathroom. I cut up lines for her.

"You're not taking any?" Her speech was slurring at this point.

"He won't let me. It's cool."

She sniffed the lines, holding onto my arm tightly to steady her hand while she held the tiny straw.

Later, I went to make a phone call. I wanted to check on Seely. We talked for ten minutes or so and I promised to come take her out the next day. I went to the bathroom and after peeing, reapplied my bright red lipstick. I went to the bar and Colleen and Armando were gone.

I stood in shock a few minutes, my mind racing for a logical explanation. I looked outside, they weren't there, but both their cars were. I waited a few minutes then tried to ask the bartender where they went. He did not speak enough English to answer me. Suddenly, I had a bad feeling. I walked outside and started walking to Armando's house, which was only two blocks away.

The lights were on, but the curtains drawn. I rang the doorbell over and over. No one answered. I tried the door, but it was locked. Just when I let go of the storm door, Armando opened the door with no shirt on.

"Negrita, baby, come in."

As I walked through the door, Colleen came past me disheveled and in a huff, only looking at Armando.

"Listen, prick, give me back my bra when you find it," she said. Then she pushed past us and stalked up the street. I ran into the living room, searching for the bra.

"Negrita, stop it. We are just drunk."

Digging into the couch, I pulled a black lacy bra out from under the cushions.

"That is from Lourdes," Armando said while giggling.

"You think this is funny, maricón. You're an asshole!" I ran at him, punching and swinging and he crouched down in defense, shielding himself with his arm from my blows. He was still laughing. I kicked him hard in his side.

"Hey, that hurts," he said.

I ran out the front door and went to my car, bra in hand. Armando tried to chase me but went back inside his house to get a shirt. I started my Nova and floored it, racing across town, breaking all my own safety rules.

Colleen was at the door of her townhouse, fumbling with the keys. I pulled up, parked next to her, and ran out of my car leaving the door open. She rushed inside trying to slam the door on me. I forced my way in and pushed her on the floor. I jumped on her and we rolled, screaming at each other, pulling hair and slapping, but not punching or scratching. There was something tame in our fight, even theatrical. She jumped up and tossed a standing metal lamp at me while she rushed to lock herself in her bedroom. I pushed the door open and shoved her on the bed. Straddling her and holding her arms down, I was screaming at her, "Why? Why, you fucking whore? Why?"

"Girlfriend, I'm sorry, I'm so fucked up. All that coke … and he never left me alone."

"You're a liar. You flirted with him all night at the bar. You're a slut." But when I raised my hand to slap her face, I hesitated.

"I love you, you know," I said. I climbed off her and left the room. She followed me into the living room and pulled on my arm.

"They're just fucking men, chica, fuck them. Sleep here. You're drunk, okay? Here, take one of these." She held out a box of truffles. "Esteban gave them to me."

I took one, and bit into the rich chocolate. She pulled me by the hand into her bedroom. "Here, put this on." She tossed me a silky black nightgown. "I'll wear the red," she said. She left the room and came back with a bottle of scotch. "Let's have a nightcap. And roll us a joint."

We got into her bed and ate candy, drank scotch from the bottle, and passed a joint. We talked about mundane things, like what we wanted to eat for breakfast. She turned off the lights and we lay together spooning. Her back was towards me and she snuggled up close, placing my hand around her waist. I held her tight.

Thirteen

Main Street ran through the center of town. It was four-lanes wide, the antithesis of the narrow one-way side streets surrounding it. It was crowded with jewelry stores, thrift shops, bodegas, and pawnshops. At the far end of Main Street, just before you reached the river and the Downtown Hotel, was the lone gun and weapons store.

The Downtown Hotel was infamous. It was a crumbling, monolithic mansion that rented rooms by the hour. Once grand, it had been built by a rich Victorian, likely a factory owner. It had the best views in town, and was situated far enough from its neighbors to operate mostly out of sight, though when you drove past there was no doubt as to what went on there. Hookers, dressed in miniskirts and sheer tops, walked back and forth in the middle of the street attempting to make eye contact with you. They clustered around the entrance to the hotel or lolled against the wall smoking cigarettes. We called them streetwalkers.

I looked at them with fascination. All I could think of was Angela and how she was murdered. What gave these girls the courage to get into cars with strange men? I looked for girls that I had met in jail, but I didn't see any of them.

After stopping at the gun shop and buying three cans of mace, I called Seely from a phone booth outside the store.

"Seely, you want to come and see my new apartment? I just rented it."

"Yeah, I'd love to."

"Okay, walk to Main Street and meet me at the gun shop."

Seely walked in while I was discussing the merits of a shotgun verses a handgun with the owner, who was trying to sell me a gun I wouldn't need a permit to buy. It was a shotgun with a sixteen-inch barrel, the shortest barrel legally allowed. Seely was quiet while I made my purchase, pulling cash from a bank envelope I got from a local bank. I had no bank account, but I always had bank envelopes. It made the cash I carried look less suspicious.

I walked to my Nova, Seely trailing behind.

"Sissy, why are you getting a gun?"

"Safety. I got you something too, here." I handed her a can of mace.

"What is it?"

"I'll show you how to use it. You should always carry it in your pocket. Remember what happened to Angela? The world is full of assholes."

I opened the back door of the Nova and slid the large cardboard box containing the disassembled gun into the backseat. Seely got in front and we drove the four blocks to my new apartment.

I now lived in an old but restored mansion from the last century. In my mind, all Edith Wharton novels took place in houses like this one. The dual front doors were heavy wood, each with a thick pane of glass in the center. The entranceway held an ancient chandelier with a push button light switch.

92

We went up two flights of steep stairs clutching thick, carved wood banisters. Reaching the top floor, I opened the door and showed off my new apartment.

Seely said, "Holy shit, this is the nicest place I've ever seen!"

We walked down a long hallway lined with newly refinished wood floors. The bedroom on the far end of the hall had a slanted ceiling on one side and tall windows on the other. A huge closet took up one wall. The living room on the opposite end of the apartment had stunning views of the river half a mile away. The kitchen was sparkling white with brand-new appliances and a charming black-and-white checkered tile floor. Every fixture in the bathroom was virgin.

"How did you rent this place, sis?"

"Come on, you know your sister is a master con-artist. How many times did I call the school pretending to be mom?"

"Who's the landlord?"

"He lives in Florida. I rented it from a real estate agent and told her I had a trust fund and my parents' lawyers would pay my rent. She kissed my ass, practically begged me to rent it. It may be renovated, but it is still a bad neighborhood. Mill Street is only two blocks away."

Mill Street, which we always called "Kill Street," was where most shootings took place. Even the cops avoided it. I used to buy drugs there sometimes, before I met Jamal. It was scary as hell.

"When you moving in?"

"Next week. You wanna go shopping for furniture with me?"

"Okay." Then she was awash with tears.

"What's wrong?"

"Nothing, I'm just scared. I don't know why, I can't explain it, I'm just afraid something bad will happen."

I got her some tissues from the bathroom calling down the hall, "Is your boy good to you?"

"Yes, he really loves me. So does Alice, I'm like her daughter. But what happened to our family?"

"We don't have one."

"But Mom used to say I was her favorite."

"Mom is a cold-hearted bitch you should forget about. You got a nice guy, you're in school, and you live with a real family."

I wanted to be more soothing, but I had stopped crying years ago. Zack always told me how unattractive it made me, and besides when I started drinking regularly at age twelve my crying jags seemed to stop altogether.

"Seely, you want a drink?"

"Yes, please."

I gave her vodka. She got so drunk I had to walk her to the door of her house hours later. Alice frowned at me, the bad older sister.

The next week, I hired moving men to move all my stuff. I felt rich. Plus, I ate out every night, usually with Armando. When he was on trips, I got takeout or ate out with Colleen. I completely ceased cooking and food shopping. I even started paying Joan to clean my apartment and do my laundry. I still hated her, but I hated domestic work also. I wanted a maid. She wouldn't steal from me, and she knew what I did for money. I could just give her my key and not worry. I kept most of my cash in a safe anyway.

Joan acted proud of me, as if she had anything to do with where I was. Eventually, Armando hired her to clean his house while he was in Florida each week. She would grab crisp hundred-dollar bills from us with huge eyes. Under-the-table cash was her favorite form of earning, and despite her simple-mindedness, she knew how to keep her mouth shut. She was excellent at lying and stonewalling, and she regarded cops and government officials as scum.

I called Colleen to come see my new apartment. Her and Seely went shopping with me while I dropped thousands on all new furniture. Colleen and I were closer than ever after that strange night. She now knew where I got my money. I mostly kept her and Armando apart, but when they were together, they were both on their best behavior. She and I never spoke about what happened. He and I did.

The day after that drunken jaunt I said to Armando, "Listen maricón, I'll stab you in your sleep if you ever ditch me in a bar again. Don't disrespect me like that."

He laughed. "Come on. It was nothing. Don't be *loca*."

"You know I always carry a hunting knife."

His face grew dark and serious, cloudy shadows moved through his eyes. "Do not threaten me. I can make you pray you were not born, *perra de mierda!*"

He stared at me, daring me to speak. I was silent.

Later, Armando handed me his written schedule. That was my cue to call the airlines and reserve his tickets. I did so dutifully, and informed him. His responses were cool and perfunctory. We hardly spoke the rest of that day.

That night, as I got dressed to go out with Armando, my stereo blasted Sheila E. singing "The Glamorous Life." I sang along with passion. All I wanted was to have that life, to be rich and ride in limos, to buy fancy clothes and jewelry, and to not need a man, really, to not need anyone. I didn't think much about my life beyond that.

Her album cover was propped up on my makeup table. She smiled slyly while she squeezed her fur coat closed near her neck. I looked at her while I did my makeup. Armando had said we were going to a new nightclub, so I wore a thin white silk blouse with a black leather miniskirt, dark nylons, and white pumps. I spent hours doing my hair and makeup to perfection. I sprayed nearly a whole can of Aquanet on my hair to make it stand up high. I wore multiple gold chains, one with my initial dangling on it, and bright gold rings on nearly every finger. Most were bought in New York City's gold district, where Armando and I went to shop sometimes. We also went to Canal Street for designer clothes and to the West Village for records.

Armando picked me up and we went to dinner as usual at Las Casa. Afterwards, he drove us to The Disco Lounge.

"Listen, muñeca, I want you to turn the owner on. His name is Rob. We'll go to his private office."

"Got it."

At the door, two huge men, obviously bouncers, stopped us. Armando whispered something to one of them. He left and returned in minutes with Rob, a lanky man with tiny eyes and thinning hair. Rob escorted us inside the club and up a set of stairs that led to his office.

"It is so nice to meet you, Armando has told me so much about you. Here, sit down." Rob offered me a seat. He was affable and smiley.

There were couches and a coffee table, like a private living room. Armando said he was going to get us drinks. I took out my kit and began cutting lines for Rob.

Armando came back with a sexy blonde waitress who had our drinks on a tray. He offered her a line and she bent over and sniffed one, and then she looked up at me.

"I'm Sherry, honey, nice to meet you." Her smile was warm and sincere, and I instantly liked her. No pretense at all, despite the fact that she was a total bombshell.

"Have another," Armando offered and she did.

Then she kissed me on the cheek saying, "Thanks, honey," and raced back downstairs to the packed bar.

"This stuff is amazing," Rob said, tilting his head back and sniffing hard to get all the coke up his nose. "You two are VIPs. Come up here whenever you want. I'll tell the bouncers you always walk right in, and at the bar, you cut to the front of the line. You guys are gonna make this place fly!"

He went to get us more drinks.

"Armando, what does he mean?"

"Negrita, we're gonna get a new customer. He'll supply this whole place and we can party here every night. You love dancing, it will be fun."

Rob returned with one of the bouncers, an All-American looking football player type named Conner. He was handsome, and huge, with thick blonde hair.

"Negrita, you and Conner should talk," said Armando, and in moments, we were alone.

I offered him a line and he snorted it like a pro.

"Your man told me you could get me an ounce. How much?"

"Fifteen," I answered, excited at the thought of a new customer.

"Can I come see you, or what?"

"Give me your address, I'll bring it over tomorrow."

"Cool. Can you come over before my shift here starts? I want to break it up and bring it with me. I think I can sell a lot here."

I wrote Conner's name and address in code in my book. "I'll be there around four?"

"Great." He left and I sat alone for a minute, sipping my daiquiri. Rob came back in.

"Can I smoke pot here?" I asked him.

"Sure, make yourself at home," he said.

As I rolled my joint, an adorable, sprightly man came bounding up the steps. His dark hair was cut at an angle, so a big piece covered his face hiding one eye. He was lively and chatty, and he told me his name was Tommy.

"I heard they're might be some lines here."

"Sure, Tommy, here you go."

He snorted up the lines with glee, and then he jumped up and down. "Girlfriend, thank you. Listen, I'm the DJ. I'll play anything you want. Request?"

"Anything by Madonna, she's my total favorite."

"You got it!" He raced back down the stairs.

I hid my purse under the couch, taking my kit out, and I left my jacket on the sofa. I went down the stairs and walked toward the dance floor. Armando was chatting up some girl but I ignored him. I stopped by the DJ booth and said, "Tommy, here," tossing him my kit.

"Oh, I love you! He grabbed me around the waist. "Here's your song, go dance."

I danced for hours under the sparkling lights of the spinning, glittering disco ball.

Armando dropped drinks off for me at the DJ booth, sometimes stopping to pinch my ass or kiss me. "Negrita, when are you going to get tired? You didn't take coke, did you?"

"No, I just love to dance! It's always been my favorite thing. I had a dance studio in my father's house."

"Well, don't leave me alone forever."

"Come dance with me," I called out to Armando but he was gone and Chaka Khan was playing. Tommy looked up at me from behind the Plexiglas and smiled while flipping his hair back with his hand. Suddenly, I realized he was gay. He was a flaming homosexual. And I was in love with him, and the music, and Sherry and Conner and Rob. I loved them all. I felt a new phase of my life beginning, maybe the life of glamour I so longed for.

Fourteen

May 1985

Age 16

Armando and I went to La Casa a few times a week. The waitresses now fought over who would serve us. Armando always left a cool hundred-dollar bill on the table, no matter it was usually a 100 percent tip. He wanted VIP treatment.

Tonight, we ate steaks and drank a bottle of champagne. During dinner, Armando passed me a small box.

"A present for you, negrita."

I opened the box to find a small black plastic square with a clip on the back. I had no idea what it was.

"It's a beeperator," Armando said.

"A what?"

"It is called a beeper. Someone calls you from their phone, they type their number in, and it comes up on the little, um, window. It vibrates when you get a call, that's why I call it a beeperator. It is like a vibrator. I'll show you, I'm gonna go call you from the phone booth."

In a minute, the thing shook itself on the table, and on the small screen appeared a phone number.

"Now we can always be in touch, plus our customers can call you on it. Oh, you can make it beep instead of vibrate."

I clipped it onto my purse in beep mode. Before long, I was tossing it down the stairs in frustration. I also once threw it out a window while drunk. That thing beeped all day and night.

We went to The Disco Lounge next, as we now did most every night while Armando was home. I also came here while he was away. I lived each day for the party that emerged at night, when I dressed up in miniskirts and skimpy tops, accented by gobs of gold jewelry. I sat at my dressing table in front of the lighted mirror for hours doing my hair and makeup while I blasted Madonna and smoked pot. Later, I danced for endless hours, not thinking about anything.

Conner pulled me aside while I was approaching the bar for a drink. "Listen, I have a friend I want you to meet. He is totally cool but he is too high up for me, he should buy straight from you."

"Do you want a cut, sweetie?"

"Nah. It's cool. Listen, people say he's in the mob, so don't ever talk about him. That's him, over at the end of the bar."

We both looked, and a man nodded at us and lifted his glass slightly.

"The black guy?"

"Yeah."

"A black guy in the mob? I thought the mob were, like, racist Italians."

"They are. I think he's working for them as muscle."

"Come on Conner … he sounds creepy"

"Don't worry, I played football with him in high school. He's alright."

I followed Conner across the bar and he introduced me to Tyrone.

"Nice to meet you," he said, taking my hand and kissing it. "May I buy you a drink?"

100

"Sure, I'll take a strawberry daiquiri."

Conner walked away, returning to his job at the door. I sat on the stool next to Tyrone.

"Conner says you might be able to hook me up."

"Yeah, I'm your girl. I'll give you my number."

He was handsome and unusually calm—almost serene. He spoke softly, but with clear self-confidence. I was instantly smitten.

Armando left town a few days later and Conner called me that same night asking for a delivery. The Disco Lounge was closed, so I was glad to get out. At his apartment, we sat watching TV and drinking peppermint schnapps after we finished our deal.

"Where's Armando?"

"Out of town."

"Oh." He switched the TV off with the remote.

"What are you doing?"

"This," he said, and he kissed me. I knew he had a crush on me, but most of my customers did. I never thought he'd act on it. His kisses were passionate, and I was alone. My boyfriend was with his wife. So I returned his kisses. I found myself melting into his hands.

I pulled myself free, "Conner, listen, if Armando found out ... we would be so screwed."

"He won't find out." He pawed at my shirt, pulling it off.

"Conner, I'm serious."

"I am too." He started undoing his belt.

"Are you crazy? If we have sex, he'll kill us both!"

"Then we won't have sex, you can just give me a blowjob," he said, pulling me towards him.

I decided to buy a car. I went to the dealer where Armando got his Camaro, mentioning his name. I asked for a good used Camaro, and bought a black one for four thousand dollars—cash. Now Armando and me had matching cars, only his was spanking new. When he came back from Florida, I told him we were going to start taking separate cars.

"Don't be loca," Armando said when I told him I wanted us to caravan places.

"Unless we are in the limo, I don't want to drive with you."

"You will do as I say."

"No, I won't, and you can't make me. I bought my own car. I work for my rent. You don't own me."

"No, but I'll punch you in your face anyway."

I walked across the living room of his house and stood in front of him.

"Go ahead, cabrón, hit me."

Armando lifted his right arm and pulled it back into a fist. We stared at each other. He dropped his fist and walked away cursing. He stomped upstairs to his bedroom and slammed the door. I turned on his television and watched MTV, hoping to see Madonna. She came on shortly, as her music videos played a few times an hour. I sang along.

I didn't always drive separate from Armando after that day. Sometimes I gave in and drove with him. But tonight I drove myself to The Disco Lounge, telling Armando I couldn't make dinner because I had work. It was humid, so I blasted the AC in my Camaro. I made my deliveries, and arrived at the club before him. I sat upstairs in the owner's lounge, cutting up lines for Tommy and Sherry. Tommy sat with his arms around me, kissing my cheeks and playing with my jewelry. Because he was gay, he was the only man Armando allowed me to touch. We were often in a clutch.

I heard footsteps on the stairs. It was Armando, breathless, and with bruises and scratches on his face.

I ran over to him. "Oh my god, are you alright? What the fuck? Did someone beat you up?"

Everyone crowded around. Sherry offered to go get some Scotch. I led Armando to the couch and he sat down. Tommy ran downstairs and came back with a cloth and a bucket of ice. I dabbed at Armando's cuts while asking what happened. His shirt was torn up, a bloody patch on the elbow. He was so shaken that he didn't speak.

After drinking some Scotch, he looked at me with puppy eyes. "I totaled the Camaro, I hit a tree. The stop sign came out of nowhere, I swear. I slammed on my brakes, but I could not stop. You need to go there. Have Conner go with you. See if the cops are there. Are you clean?"

I tossed my kit on the table. "Now I am."

Conner and I drove to the address Armando gave us. There were no cops, just an empty field with a huge oak tree and a pile of metal under it that had once been the Camaro.

"How did he live through this?" Conner asked.

"He told me he opened the door and rolled out once he knew he was gonna crash."

"Shit, look at those skid marks. He was probably going eighty."

"Yup."

"But this is a 15 mile-an-hour neighborhood. He's such an asshole!"

"Yes, he is. Especially behind the wheel."

We got back in the car and drove back towards the club. When I stopped at the next sign, Conner leaned over to kiss me. We briefly made out.

"I'm not going to leave him."

"Why?"

"I love him. Plus, he'll kill us. Mira, we need to get back and call a tow truck."

We went back to The Lounge and gave the report. Rob handed me a phone book and his business phone. We had the car towed away before anyone called the police.

The next day Armando bought a brand-new red Camaro IROC-Z.

Fifteen

Jacked: To take something illicitly; steal

"Negrita, book two tickets. You are coming to Miami with me." Armando called to me from the shower.

I was propped up on a pillow while lying across his bed. With the phone and my notebook, I was playing travel agent as I always did. I didn't mess up numbers the way he did.

"I've never been on a plane before, mi amor. Can we go first class?"

"No. It will draw too much attention."

He was right, of course.

"Well what about Lourdes, does she know I'm coming?"

"No, she is in Puerto Rico for one month, to see her mamá."

We drove to JFK a week later on a balmy afternoon. The ride was typical. I yelled at Armando whenever he pulled a boneheaded move on the road. He laughed and said I was silly. I used the mirror on the back of my visor to pass the time by applying face powder and lipstick.

We parked and took a shuttle to the airline terminal. Armando approached the counter.

"Tickets for Mr. and Mrs. Hernandez, por fav—uh, please."

The receptionist began typing. She glanced at him and smiled and he nodded through half-closed lids.

"I like your necklace," he said to her, "pearls?"

"Yes, they were my grandmother's," she answered, lowering her eyes back towards the computer screen.

I stood quietly and mashed Armando's foot with the pointy toe of my shoe. He struggled to free his shoe from under mine. When the receptionist presented our tickets, Armando flashed her a seductive grin, and touched her hand as he took them. She was clearly flummoxed.

As we walked away I said, "Why do you always have to be such a chulo?"

"Because you are such a perra," he answered, striding toward a shoeshine stand. "Look what you did to my Gucci's." He sat scowling while an elderly man rubbed off the scuff marks I had made on the black leather.

Once seated on the plane I pressed my nose to the glass, watching the ascent over New York City. The buildings grew smaller and smaller, and soon we were sailing through clouds and ordering drinks.

"Let's fuck in the bathroom," Armando said.

"No way, cabrón."

"Come on, por qué?" He placed my hand in his lap so I could feel his hard-on.

I quickly pulled my hand away. "Why don't you ask the stewardess?"

He called her over and I held my breath. He simply ordered two more drinks. By the time we landed, we both stumbled off the plane drunk.

We walked outside the airport, pushing through a thick wall of humidity. I could feel my foundation melting as streams of sweat poured down my face. The temperature was over ninety degrees. The humidity was unbearable. I followed Armando as he led me through the parking lot to a large black sedan. We threw our bags in the backseat and drove off, the air conditioner on full blast.

He drove us to a tiny tract house in a newly built development. A large white boat sat on a trailer to the right of the garage. He drove into the garage using an automatic opener. The door rattled shut behind us as we walked through an interior door into the kitchen. The house was sparsely furnished. The dining room was completely empty. The living room only contained a large tan sofa and a big screen TV. As usual, there were no decorations or knick-knacks.

It was the opposite of my apartment, where polished cherry tables sat at each end of the plush, brand-new white sofa. A white recliner under a brass standing lamp sat adjacent. Matching cut-glass table lamps, framed posters of Van Gogh's sunflowers, and fancy porcelain vases filled with fresh flowers made my friends say my place looked like it could be in a magazine.

"Why isn't there any furniture?" I asked Armando.

"Qué?"

"Why all this empty space?"

He shrugged. I figured he must prefer to spend his money on cars and boats. He fiddled with the thermostat and the central air kicked on, pumping cool air into the stuffy, sealed house.

"Aquí, I'll show you some furniture." He took my hand and led me down the thickly carpeted hallway to his bedroom. He pushed me on the bed.

"No, it's too hot."

"Take off your clothes," he said, kneeling down to pull my shoes off, tossing them one after the other across the room. "Now, tranquilo, mi amor."

Later, while Armando showered, I looked through his dresser drawers. One drawer was lined on the bottom with a white hotel towel. A half a dozen handguns lay on top. I picked up a boxy silver one and held it up, pointing it at the mirror.

"Whoa, Negrita, careful." Armando appeared in the glass behind me wearing only a towel around his waist. He reached around me with his arm outstretched, placing his hand over mine and straightening my aim. He rested his head on my shoulder. "Now, pull."

I did, and the glass shattered. Armando laughed heartily.

"Marricón! I didn't know it was loaded."

"All of them are."

"But we just shot a hole in the wall."

"So?" he said, picking up another gun and firing it over top of the broken mirror, making another hole in the wall.

Armando had two men join us for dinner. The three of them spoke Spanish, leaving me to daydream while looking out at the ocean and drinking glass after glass of red wine.

We both got drunk for the second time that day. After the men left, we drove a few blocks and stumbled onto the beach, falling down and laughing. We lay on the sand looking up at the half-moon hanging low over the water.

"Negrita, I love you," Armando said.

"Me too. I love you."

"Do you swear?"

"I swear."

"Good. Because if I find out you are kissing some guy, I'm going to kill you. And him."

"Why are you always talking about other guys?"

"You lie, chica. You are a liar *profesional*, a *traficante*. But if you lie to me, I will find out. And you will regret it the rest of your life."

We lay in silence for a time.

"You're paranoid," I said.

We walked hand in hand to the sedan and drove back to his house. Once inside he turned on the TV and handed me the remote. "Watch something, I'm going out a little while."

I watched MTV for hours, until I was seeing all the same videos again and again. I went into Armando's bed and woke up when he was crawling in beside me.

"Where were you?" I asked him.

"Working. Now sleep." He wrapped his arms around me, clutching me tightly.

In the morning, I found him sitting at the cheap Formica kitchen table drinking a cup of strong Cuban coffee. He was shirtless, wearing only striped men's pajama bottoms. I thought he looked hunky without a shirt; he was slender with toned, muscular arms and rich cocoa skin.

"What are we doing today?" I asked. I hugged him from behind then sat with him at the table, refusing coffee and lighting a cigarette instead.

"Today? Today we go on the ocean."

"With your new boat?"

"Sí."

We fought over who would drive the boat, as I grew up driving my father's boats on the river. He won and he drove the boat demonically fast, even though there were posted speed limit signs since we were in a bay. Finally, a pretty female coast guard pulled us over with a siren. She wrote Armando a ticket. I was secretly glad. Whether on land or water he drove like an asshole. He apologized profusely to the officer, turning on his usual charm. Once she left, he crumpled up the ticket and tossed it into the sea.

When it was time to go back to New York, Armando told me we would fly separately.

"Why?" I said, "por qué?"

Armando glared at me. "You will meet me at the airport, chica, I will be there soon after you. Have some food and wait."

I asked no more questions. It would only make him angry, and besides, it gave me a chance to fly on a plane alone. None of my friends had ever done that, and once onboard, I ordered a white wine and was served without being asked for ID.

When we walked out of JFK, bags in hand, I relaxed for the first time that day. Once we paid the parking fee and he drove onto the expressway, Armando sighed loudly.

"Are you okay, Armando?"

"Si. I brought us something back."

"But you only had carry-on! How did you get it through the x-ray?"

"Same as always, I wrap it up, like for a birthday."

"But I didn't know you put it in your carryon. What does it look like on the screen?"

"Like a box … it looks fine."

"No one asked you what it was?"

"No."

"Were you nervous?"

"Nah… well, un poquito."

"Well, I'm scared now."

"Chica, forget it. Don't think. We are driving home, that is all. We must now get it to the safe without being jacked."

We reached Southbridge late that night. Armando parked the IROC-Z in a private parking lot behind a house on the next street.

"Hold this." He pulled a loaded 9mm handgun out of the glove box and passed it to me. We climbed out of the car. He reached into the backseat and grabbed our bags.

"Negrita, put the gun in your pocket, in case."

"I can't, Armando, my pants are too tight."

The Jordache jeans I wore were purposely one size too small. I had to lay flat on my bed to zipper them. Other than that, I had a skimpy cotton halter-top that hid nothing, and white pumps. Armando's eyes drifted over me, coming to rest on my large, white leather purse.

"Okay. Leave your purse over your shoulder, put the gun inside, and put your hand … *como se dice* … ahh … *suavemente?*" He lifted his hand to demonstrate.

"Lightly." I now taught him words without even thinking.

"Sí, Sí, lightly on top of your purse. Don't close it."

We walked calmly down the faintly lit sidewalks. It was quiet for a warm summer night. Fans hummed in dark windows, sending a slight breeze as we walked past. We could hear the faint clamor of talking and jukebox music from *Descansar*, the tiny bar on the next block.

When we reached Armando's door, we both drew deep breaths of relief. Neither cops nor robbers had ambushed us.

Once inside, we walked straight up the narrow wooden staircase to the second floor without turning any lights on. We went into Armando's bedroom, closing and locking the door. The shades were already drawn. Armando opened the closet door and then the safe. He unzipped his suitcase, and dug through his clothes for the ki. He ripped the wrapping paper off the box and pulled the brick from inside, shaking the tissue paper off. He placed the ki inside and closed the safe.

"We'll break it mañana. Let's go to the Descansar."

We stayed until after they closed, laying out lines on the bar for the owner and the bartender.

The next day as I dressed to make my rounds, Armando sat on his bed looking thoughtful.

"Chica, I won't be doing that again."

"What?"

"I shouldn't be carrying, and you cannot do it, I need you here. Do you know any girls that will do it?"

"I'll think about it."

"What about Seely?"

"Never."

"Okay. Maybe Colleen?"

"Why does it have to be my friend?"

"It has to be a white girl. And someone smart who won't talk if they get caught."

"Lemme think about it." I kissed him goodbye and left. Business was continuing to grow and by dinner, I had sold almost half the kilo.

A week later Lourdes returned and Armando flew to Florida to see her and José. I called Colleen and Seely, asking them to go to dinner and to The Disco Lounge with me. I picked them up in my Camaro. We went to La Casa, and ordered plates of shrimp and lobster. We also drank two bottles of wine. Seely, now fifteen, wasn't even asked for ID.

When we arrived at The Lounge, Conner summoned us to the front of the long line. There was an entry fee, but we didn't have to pay it. The girl in the booth smiled and waved hello to us. The people waiting on line stared at us with a mix of anger and curiosity. I felt like a celebrity.

I rushed to the DJ booth and jumped into Tommy's arms. He gave me a full, wet kiss. I handed him my kit, and he promptly started spinning all my favorite songs. Colleen fetched me shots of Schnapps and handed them to me on the dance floor. After dancing awhile I grabbed my kit back from Tommy. Colleen, Seely and I went into the bathroom and I sat in the lounge area, where I often held court. I laid out lines for them both, warning Seely to go lightly.

"I know. I've done it a bunch of times," she said.

"What do you mean?"

"Armando gave some to Mike a few times."

Drunk, I started ranting that I would kick her ass if she got hooked. I also issued death threats towards Armando. Finally, Colleen told me to shut the fuck up.

"Fine, puta, *chinga tu madre!*"

"Fuck your mother, bitch," she said back.

With that, I got up from the plush gold chair of the powder room and threw my drink at Colleen. She kicked me and I grabbed her hair.

"Get the fuck off of me, puta," she screamed.

Seely burst into tears.

"I'm getting more drinks, this is bullshit!" I stalked out of the ladies room to see Conner talking to a sexy blonde. I walked up to them.

"Excuse me," I said.

Conner told the girl to wait a minute. He held my arm and walked me a few steps away.

"What's up?" he said.

"Who's the girl?"

"Melissa. Can I go now?"

"Yeah, fuck you asshole." I walked away and Conner called after me, "Sleep it off, girl."

I leaned over the bar and asked Sherry to give me a bottle of champagne and three glasses. I heard a man say my name, and I turned around to see a gorgeous guy with blonde feathered hair.

"Yes?"

"I'm Ryan, remember me? I'm Jay's older brother." He smiled sweetly. He seemed kind of shy.

"Oh yeah, how is Jay?" Jay was a high school customer of mine. I delivered to his house a few times and met Ryan there once.

"He's good ... so listen, what are you up to right now? Can we have drink?"

I grabbed the champagne bottle and glasses off the bar.

"Come on," I said.

I led him into the ladies room. He hesitated, but I insisted. I put him in a chair and sat on his lap, introducing him to Seely and Colleen and pouring champagne for all. I drank straight from the bottle. Conner came to the swinging door and opened it just a crack, calling my name.

"What?"

"You know you can't have a guy in there."

I went over and pushed the door shut on him, laughing.

"She's really drunk," Colleen said.

"Shut up *idiota*," I said.

"Seriously, girlfriend, you can't drive."

"Fine, Ryan will drive me, won't you?"

"Sure," he said.

Later, when Seely insisted she had to get home, Colleen, Seely, Ryan and I all piled into the Camaro. I gave Ryan the keys.

"What about my car?" he asked.

"I'll drive you back tomorrow."

"Okay," he said. I sat in the front passenger seat and gave Ryan directions. First we took Seely to her house. I got out with her and hugged her on unsteady feet, until Colleen got out and dragged me back into the car. When we got to her house, she asked Ryan to take care of me before she got out.

"Ignore her, I'm perfectly fine," I said, and then I kissed her, promising her I was okay.

Ryan drove to my apartment. I led him upstairs and he used my keys to open the door.

"Holy shit, this is your place?"

"Yeah."

"So it's true … I heard you were selling coke now, that's why I wanted to talk to you. I want some."

"No problema, but can we talk in the morning?"

"Sure."

I led him down the dark hallway to my bedroom. We made out on my bed until we both passed out. We slept fully clothed on top of the covers.

When I woke up, I called the restaurant on Main Street, and ordered breakfast to be delivered.

"So," Ryan said, "I want to talk to you about coke, but I also want to know if you're free for dinner."

"Sweetie, I'd love to. But I have a boyfriend who's insanely jealous."

"Oh, I didn't know."

"Don't worry, he's out of town. How about coming here tonight instead?"

Sixteen

July 1985

Age 17

Safe House: A house where a dealer can store drugs, money and other contraband in a heavy safe. The owner of the house is paid a monthly fee. The owner is a neutral party and cannot be a dealer or involved in any illegal business. His house must be "cool". Large amounts of contraband are rarely stored in the home of a dealer once he can afford a safe house.

When Armando was in town, we went out every night. He would call to plead for me to be ready to go when he arrived. I was never ready. I gave him a key so he could let himself in while my music was blasting.

I was dancing in my living room with my hair still wet, playing my latest favorite song "In the Evening," by Sheryl Lee Ralph. It's about a woman who turns into her true self at night. She says she lives like a star, and though she can't explain it, it helps her survive. I feel the exact same way. When I dress up and go to the disco, I feel more myself than any other time. And my life, which often feels scary and confusing, drifts away while I dance. It's just the music and me, as if nothing else exists.

Armando interrupted my solo dance by turning the music off. I was startled, I never heard him come in.

"Negrita, why are you dancing in your house? You are so funny." He was chuckling.

"I always do. I had a dance room at my father's."

"You dance too much," he said. He walked across the room and casually began to search for something in my purse.

"What are you doing?"

"Ah, waiting for you, *de prisa*, let's go."

"No, what are doing in my purse?"

He looked up with the guilty face of a little boy. "I just need a pen. I always look in Lourdes's bag."

"We'll, she's your wife and I'm not."

"But you are my partner."

"Really? Then why am I only making five-thousand dollars a month, when the coke sales are making thirty-five thousand?"

"I have a son and wife to support."

"Well, I have myself to support and I need to hire a driver and get a safe house."

"Sí, sí. I really cannot go into your bag? Why? What do you hide from me?"

"Nothing!"

I finished blow-drying and curling my hair, then sprayed it stiff with hairspray that was practically shellac. My sleeveless stretchy red dress was blousy on top, and form fitting at the waist. It was short, stopping at the tops of my thighs. I wriggled into tight black nylon stockings and stepped into shiny red pumps.

"I'm taking my own car," I said.

"Mierda! Every night with this. I am driving you!"

Some nights I won this fight and we went everywhere as a convoy. Tonight, I agreed to drive with him. I was nervous that I had banned him from my purse. I didn't know why I did it. I wasn't hiding anything from him, at least not in my purse. All it would do was make him more suspicious. He had already taken to returning from trips on different days and times than he told me in our daily calls, and then surprising me at my apartment.

Armando drove us to the La Casa. We ate lobster and filet mignon and drank Dom Pérignon. Almost every time we came here, we ate the same food and drank the same drink. We had a mutual penchant for routine. By eleven o'clock, we had arrived at The Disco Lounge, where we were welcomed like celebrities.

In a tiny radius of five miles, we sold our coke, ate our meals, drank at three different bars and partied at a disco.

And I told nothing of my layered, secret life to anyone. The houses I visited, the closet full of coke, the briefcases full of money, the bikers, the teenage boys I kissed, these were all things I spoke of to no one, not even to Seely or Colleen.

A few days later Armando went back to Florida. I spent the day answering pages, and driving my deliveries around in my Camaro. I went to see Conner, and neither of us mentioned Melissa.

"Is Armando around?" Conner asked.

"He just left town today."

"Good, then come're."

We made out on his couch while the TV played a football game in the background.

"Come to my bed," he said.

"You know I can't."

"Why? He's away, he'll never know."

"It's just one of my rules. I can't go all the way with any man but him. Somehow I know if I do, he'll find out."

"Your rules are stupid."

"Yeah, well so are you. He has crazy guns, and you know he's reckless."

"Fine, just don't give me shit for having a girlfriend."

"That bimbo is your girlfriend now?"

"Fuck you."

"Fine." I picked up the pile of money and counted it, then tossed it in my purse. "Later, loser."

"Bye, cockteaser."

I slammed the door on the way out. I knew I had no right to be jealous, but I was.

As I walked down the stairs towards my car, my pager vibrated and Seely's number came up. I drove straight to her house. She opened the door, her face streaked with tears.

"What's wrong?"

"Come to my room."

We lay on her bed together and I rolled a joint. Alice allowed her to smoke, so I lit it up and passed it to her.

"Seely, talk."

"I miss Mom, and Stan. I miss our old house and the dogs. Where did our dogs go?" She started to sob.

"Stan has them." Stan was our mother's husband for ten years. She made him move out when she met Harry.

"I want my dog back!"

She hugged a pillow, crying, and asked me to get her a can of beer from the fridge.

I fetched it, and she popped it open and drank deeply.

I wish I could say I comforted her but I did not. Instead, I scolded her for missing Joan.

"Why would you miss a cunt like that? Don't you remember how evil she was?"

"I still love her."

"Well, you're a fucking idiot."

My pager went off. It was God. I got up and grabbed my purse off the bed.

"Sweetie, I gotta go. I'm still working." I pulled out a fifty-dollar bill and gave it to her. "Here, buy yourself something. I love you."

Driving away, I burst into tears.

Later that night, I stopped at Hector's. I ran into Mateo, who was Lourdes' brother. We sat together at the bar drinking and bullshitting until last call.

The next day I called Armando at his house in Key Biscayne.

"Mira, what do you think about me hiring Mateo to drive me?"

"I think it might work. We will talk when I am back."

"When's that?"

"Soon, very soon."

"Okay. I love you."

"Me too, Negrita."

Really, I called to see if he was still in Florida, because he had not called the day before which might mean he was traveling. I wanted to see Ryan that night, so I tried to calculate if there was any way Armando might surprise me early. It was afternoon, so I decided to go to the Descansar for a few drinks. Right before I got in the shower, my pager beeped. It was Tyrone, who always came to my place. Cool, I thought, let me make a few thousand before I go out. So I called him back.

"Can I come over?" he said.

"Yeah, just give me an hour, I'm just jumping into the shower."

Tyrone knocked at my door thirty minutes later. I was showered and had dried my hair, but I was not yet dressed. I was wearing a long red silk robe. I spoke to him through the door.

"Ty, I'm still not dressed. You're early."

"Sorry, girl, let me in, I'll wait."

I opened the door and he walked in, sniggering.

"I like you undressed," he said.

"Maybe you'd like to end up with a bullet in your head?"

"I'm not scared of your man. He's candy. And I sure ain't scared of you."

"Shut up and go into the living room."

I followed him there, offered him a seat, and then turned to leave. He grabbed my hand.

"Please, sit down with me, just for a minute."

I sat down on the plush recliner. "What, Tyrone, what is so important that I can't go get dressed?"

"This," he said, and he kneeled down before me. He put one hand on each of my legs and slowly moved them up under my robe while he held my gaze. He had a beautiful face, with dark, intelligent eyes. My body started to shake, but I didn't try to move away. He leaned forward and kissed me, pulling on my bottom lip with his teeth. His hands moved up my thighs and before I could protest, he was touching me with skilled fingers. Then, my robe was open and my naked body exposed. Tyrone, still on his knees, kissed and touched me everywhere. I writhed with pleasure.

"I'm going to take you from Armando."

"No," I said. But my resolve felt weak. I wished Armando had half the skill of Tyrone.

"Babygirl, you're gonna be mine."

122

"Tyrone, you have to swear you won't tell Armando. Swear!"

"I promise. But he'll know once you are with me."

"No, I can't leave Armando, I'm sorry."

"We'll see," he said. "I always get what I want."

Seventeen

Peter came with the limo to pick me up on a sweltering summer afternoon. Armando had asked me to come get him at Newark Airport. I drank two glasses of white wine on the ride, and read Gogol's *Diary of a Madman*. I stuffed it into my purse as we pulled up to the terminal. Armando always teased me for reading books.

With a deep furrow in his brow and distant darting eyes, Armando looked worried. His movie star smile, which he was always flashing, was absent. He got into the limo and nodded hello.

"Baby, what's up? Did something bad happen?"

"Sí, sí, Negrita. I have very bad news."

"Qué?"

"It is Lourdes' brother, Carlos. He just got released from prison."

"Why is that bad?"

"He's loco. *Loco de mierda.* And *peligroso* … means, um, very dangerous."

"What did he go down for? Murder?"

"No. Armed robbery. But he has been there twelve years now and before he was in the *cárcel juvenil* for four years."

"The cárcel juvenil … you mean like a jail for juveniles?"

"Sí, sí. He is very bad. His head is all wrong."

"Why do we have to worry?"

"Chica, come on, we've got a lot of business. He is in Southbridge now, and Lourdes and her *madre* say I must help him."

"How can you help him, isn't he on parole?"

"No, he could not get parole. He escaped and they caught him. They made him stay until the finish, twelve years. We are *tan jodido*."

"¿Qué?"

"Nothing."

"Why don't you just, you know, kill him?"

"Muchacha estúpida, estúpida! He is familia; I am obligado to help him. Comprendes?"

"Sí, I do."

Armando sat stewing. He pushed me away when I tried to hug him. He had Peter drive to my apartment.

"Get dressed for dinner. I'll come back later to get you," he said.

I kissed his cheek and slid out the door Peter stood holding open for me. I gave him a wave and he tipped his hat.

As I sat at my vanity putting on makeup, I kept thinking about how Armando looked. His eyes, his creased brow, he looked … afraid. It was a look I'd never once seen on his face.

My phone rang. "Negrita, I am sending my brother Carlos to your house. Give him something on me, sí?"

"Are you fucking kidding? You're going to send a psycho to my house?"

"Gracias, chica." He hung up the phone.

"Mother fucker!" I yelled into the disconnected line.

Ten minutes later my doorbell rang. I pushed the release and in minutes a rather handsome Puerto Rican man stood in my living room. He was stout and barely more than five feet tall. He was nothing like the imposing figure I'd imagined. He beamed with a radiant smile. His black hair had wide streaks of gray and was greased back into a ponytail.

"I'm celebrating tonight, muñeca. I'm about to tear this town up!"

"Cool, well, have fun."

"Sí chica, I will. I just got out of prison a few hours ago."

"Yeah, I heard."

"I'm going to party! You want to come? You're very pretty."

"No, gracias. I have plans."

"Some other night then."

I gave him an eight-ball of coke, though he was already so amped, I could not imagine how he'd be after he got high.

"Gracias, gracias, I'll see you again. Armando gave me your pager number."

I froze at his words. He kissed my cheek while I stood holding the door.

"*Buenas noches, putaña.*" He laughed loudly and bounded down the stairs.

I shut the door and stood there fuming at Armando. The little bastard had just called me a whore.

When Armando came to get me, I ignored the buzzer and the door. He used his key and came in, calling my name down the hall.

"Go fuck yourself!" I said.

"Negrita, what is wrong?"

He came down the hall to my bedroom.

"Que?" he said.

"You know, pendejo! You tell me scary stories about that guy all the way back in the limo, then you send him to my house, to my fucking house! What's wrong with you? You are supposed to protect me!"

"I will, I promise. He won't do nothing. I told you I have to help him."

A few days later, Armando called and said, "Negrita, you must come to *mi casa. Ahora mismo*, now, right now."

I drove over and we sat in the living room.

"What's wrong mi amor?"

"I found out from some of my people that Carlos was going to rob you with a gun. Do not worry. I have fixed it. I had to tell him you were mine."

"What the fuck? Why did you send him to my house, why are you acting so *stupido*? And why didn't you tell him I was your girlfriend before, cabrón!"

"I thought it would keep you safer if he did not know, I fucked it up, I know."

"Fucked it up? I could be dead!"

"No, no. But you gotta move your coke. Get a safe house like we talked about. You should not be living with the producto anyway."

I started to cry and he put his arms around me.

"Leave me alone, I hate you!"

"Shh, muñeca. He is coming to dinner tonight with us."

"No, no fucking way!"

"Sí, and he will … uh … um … *como se dice discúlpese?*"

"No comprendo."

"He will tell you sorry."

At dinner that night Carlos was as wound up as the night I met him. He kissed my hand in the dramatic gesture of a madman. I thought of my Gogol book and pictured him being carted off as he imagined he was king of Spain.

"*Señorita*, I am so sorry. Armando told me everything. I thought you were just some dumb whore, or I would never have planned to tie you up and rob you."

I sat speechless.

"Can you forgive me?"

"Were you going to shoot me?"

"Nah, maybe just *violarte* you a little—I'm just kidding."

"What did he just say?" I asked Armando.

"Nothing, nothing, Negrita."

"Negrita, huh?" Carlos said. "How sweet. I said rape."

He continued to shovel food into his mouth rapidly while leaning over his plate. I stared at my food unable to eat. All I could think was what if Armando hadn't found out about his plot? I excused myself to the ladies room where I sat on a red velvet divan and cried into a handful of paper towels.

Back at the table, I ordered shots of peach schnapps, which I chased with a strawberry daiquiri. I pushed my plate away and tried to tune out Carlos' prison tales, which involved shanks, brawls, and a dramatic breakout. There was also a story about a shooting during a robbery where a security guard's head exploded from a bullet.

His laugh was loony, and he laughed a lot. His voice was also loud; he seemed to yell everything he said. "I'll tell you, that *pato* guard's head went everywhere, there was blood all over Manny. I told him, oh shit, motherfucker, we gonna fry for this!"

I was glad I had skipped eating, as I was now on the verge of puking. I had never heard graphic crime stories live before and though I was a news hound, I often skipped the graphic descriptions of crimes. I read

Helter Skelter the summer I was fourteen, and it gave me nightmares for weeks.

The grueling dinner finally ended, and we all got into the limo together to go to the disco.

"My man's riding in style, now," he said to Armando. Then they talked in rapid Spanish I could not understand. Armando reached for my hand but I pulled it away. I looked up and saw Carlos' eyes on my hand. He had seen me pull away. I switched seats ostensibly to ask Peter to change the music. I remained seated across from both men, my stomach in a tight knot.

When we got to the Disco Lounge I excused myself and went up to Rob's office, where I rolled a joint. On the way up, I asked Sherry to bring me a bottle of schnapps and a shot glass.

I sat in the office smoking alone. Sherry brought me the schnapps. She wore a tank top and her tousled blond hair fell on bare shoulders. She leaned over me to put the bottle on the table, and I could smell her perfume.

"You smell good," I said.

"Chanel No.5, you know, like Marilyn Monroe." Marilyn was her idol, and she talked in similar sexy baby voice.

"Honey, are you okay?"

"Sure, Sher, I'm fine." I poured myself a shot.

"I think Armando's looking for you."

"I'm sure he'll find me. Just don't tell him I'm here."

"Are you two fighting?"

"Yeah."

"I'm sorry." She gave me a tight hug and ran back down to the crowded bar.

Armando eventually came up to the office and found me.

"Why are you here, negrita? Don't you want to dance?"

130

"No, I don't"

"Come on," he said, and pulled on my arm.

"Get off me maricón, leave me alone!"

He left and I sat there drinking shot after shot of peach schnapps. I don't remember how the night ended. I only know I woke up in Armando's bed the next day with the worst hangover I'd ever had.

A few days later I went to my friend Janet's house, to propose putting a safe in her closet and keeping my cocaine and money there. She had two very young children, and a mild coke habit. She struggled as a single mother. I often brought them bags of groceries. This way, I thought, I could pay her. I offered her four hundred bucks per month, which was more than welfare would have given her. She said yes without hesitation and I left, telling her there would be a small safe delivered to her apartment later that week. I reminded her that there was risk, but we never discussed the potential consequences.

I called Zack that night. "Daddy, things are really scary."

"I'll come tomorrow," he said.

The next day, I made steak for my father as he sat at my kitchen table. I was afraid to tell him anything. We talked about his kids and my grandmother who lived with him. While we were eating he asked what I was scared of.

"I don't know. Life, I guess."

He looked thoughtful. "Listen, sweetheart, if things ever get bad, or dangerous, just run away. Show up at my door, even if you only stay one night. Just get away if you have to."

"I will, daddy."

He walked around my apartment, looking at my framed art. "I love these Van Gogh's," he said, "You have all the sunflowers paintings."

"Yes."

Then he pulled on the door to my living room.

"What the fuck is this?" He held my shotgun, which had been standing hidden behind the door.

"Protection."

He examined the gun, turning it over and opening the chamber.

"This thing is loaded. Are you out of your mind?"

"No, daddy, I need that."

"No you don't. I'm taking it with me right now."

And the bastard left with my gun, after I told him I was scared. I protested, but he overruled me. He even looked in the hall closet for the shells, and took those too. I hated him, and I hated Armando. Neither of them really cared about what happened to me.

And I was positive that one of them was going to get me killed.

Eighteen

Boot: Slang for injecting drugs with a needle.

"Bienvenidos!"

A portly middle-aged man with a thick accent greeted us as we came through the heavy wooden doors. He had thinning dark hair and a neat mustache. Three thick braided gold chains showed through his half open shirt.

As the doors closed, I saw two men standing on either side of the door facing the grand hall. Each man held a black machine gun. Each stood staring straight ahead, expressionless, like those guards outside Windsor Palace.

Armando and I had flown to Miami, and we were staying at the Hyatt in a huge suite. We were only here for two nights, and Armando did not tell Lourdes we were here. He said he needed me to come and meet some people, that he had an important meeting and it would help him if I were there.

We sat in a richly furnished living room with luxurious gold sofas and gaudy lampshades accented with braiding and tassels. Plush white carpets underscored the immaculateness. I sat on a small loveseat. Armando sat across from me on the sofa with the man who had greeted us at the door.

"Negrita, this is Lalo."

I smiled and bowed my head slightly. *"Hola, buenas tardes."*

"Buenas tardes. You … muy bonito … Rosa, en Inglés?"

A gorgeous woman with thick, dark curls breezed into the living room. "My brother says it is nice to meet you. I am Rosa, Lalo's sister."

She extended a delicate hand with long red nails. I briefly admired her garish gold rings, and then took her hand. She was laughing and calling out in Spanish to the men, who laughed with her. Then, she kissed my cheek.

"Lalo does not know English so well. He mostly stays at our family farm." She took my hand and held it, sitting down next to me on the loveseat.

"I love the country. Where is your farm?" I said.

"Oh, in Colombia, in the mountains. You would love my family's farm. It is so beautiful!"

She turned to the men and spoke Spanish to them. I could only grab the gist of what they said. They were reminiscing about Colombia.

My eyes wandered to a row of tall glass windows that looked out into the yard at a green expanse punctuated with palm trees. In the distance, I could see the brick wall that met at the iron gates we had passed through in the front. It dawned on me I was visiting a gated mansion.

I watched the men who were walking the grounds as well as lurking in the room we were in. They were all armed. They never spoke nor made direct eye contact. I thought they were sexy.

"Mi hija! What are you doing?" Armando was studying me from across the room.

"Qué?"

"You heard me." His eyes narrowed.

Rosa interrupted. "Chica let us get you a drink. You are thirsty, I'm sure. What is you're favorite?"

"Well, um, strawberry daiquiri, but anything you have is fine."

"No, no, we can make you that."

Rosa called out in Spanish for the drink, and a few minutes later a man came in and placed it before me, then disappeared.

"My cousin," she said.

Armando was still glaring. I tried to glare back, covertly. His jealousy was oppressive. He could fool around with hookers and even my best friend, but I could not even look at another man with admiration.

Soon, Rosa announced dinner. The four of us walked to the dining room, where formal place settings were laid out. She told us where to sit.

"You, chica, will sit next to me." She squeezed my hand again.

The cousin served us our dinner. Soon, I learned that everyone there was a cousin. The driver, the cook, the guards—all cousins.

Lobster was served, and Lalo cracked open the Dom Pérignon, which had been sitting in an ice bucket on the table. I wondered if this was how Armando had gotten a taste for the hundred-dollar a bottle bubbly.

As we ate, Rosa told me all about Colombia.

"Ah, chica, you must come and see my country. My family's farm is in the mountains a few hours outside Yarumal, in the north. It is so pretty, so many trees and flowers. And it is so lush."

"Rosa, your English is very good."

"Yes, well, my brothers sent me to an English language school in Bogotá, so I could help them make their way in America."

She called over to Lalo and spoke to him in Spanish. Then she said to me, "I told him, he should have learned too!"

Armando leaned over and started speaking softly to Lalo. Rosa then turned towards me.

"You know, Armando has told us so much about you, how very smart and good you are and we insisted he bring you here to meet us."

"That's nice," I smiled at Armando and he lifted his glass slightly towards me. I could feel him study me from across the table.

"Well, Lalo and I do not want to steal you from him, but we would like you to go to Colombia for a little while."

"Me? Go to Colombia?"

"Sí, chica, there is nothing to fear. You will go to our family's farm for one month. You can relax, sit in the sun, and swim. We have a pool. You can have your own rooms. Our house is very large. And you will eat the best food every day. Then, you will bring back some cocaine for us. Just a couple of suitcases, not too much."

"How will I get it past customs?"

"Oh, it's so easy. You just wear nice clothes and walk right past the customs officers. They never check the bags of white people."

"Really?"

"Oh sí. We do it all the time. And we will give you twenty thousand dollars."

"Twenty thousand?"

"Sí. It will be worth it for us. Then, maybe in a time, you will go again."

"I, um, I, I … I don't know."

"Do not worry, sweet one. You sleep on it. We will all have breakfast tomorrow, right Armando?"

136

She smiled softly, her charm and elegance lighting the room.

"Now come with me to the kitchen, chica, and we will choose dessert, eh?" She pulled me away from the table and I glanced at Armando.

He kept his composure, but in his eyes I saw those familiar shadows. He was not happy.

All night at the hotel, I thought about what Rosa had said. A brand-new Camaro was only ten thousand dollars and I really wanted one. Plus, I'd never been to a foreign country. Armando did not mention their proposal, and I was afraid to ask him about it. When we returned to the Hyatt, we sat at the hotel bar. Armando pouted and ignored me while watching the television. It was clear he would be mad if I said yes. Maybe I would even lose him. But the money … all that money!

I might lose Armando, but Rosa's cousins were handsome and young. I could get another suave, sexy South American boyfriend. I could make eighty thousand dollars a year and spend just four months working, most of it chilling in a mansion. I practically drooled daydreaming of that farm in the mountains with armed guards roaming the grounds, brown-skinned and shirtless. I was so tempted. Then there was Rosa. I only met her tonight, but I wanted to please her, to be close to her warmth, to learn how to be as sophisticated as her.

There was only one hitch to this proposal. By an odd twist of fate, I had seen the film *Midnight Express* on late night cable only weeks before. All I could think of is what would happen if I were caught in Colombia. Sure, if the Feds got me here, I could get a lawyer and bail. But what if I was thrown in a Colombian jail? I might have to eat bugs! Or get a life sentence or even the death penalty. And the jail would be filthy, rat infested, and corrupt. I knew it wasn't Turkey, but I was sure it was similar.

And that was all that made me say no.

Armando seemed cheery on the plane ride home.

"You didn't want me to go to Colombia."

"I do not want to lose my favorite girl, never."

"How come you brought me there? Did you know they were going to ask me?"

"Sí."

"And?"

"You must decide for yourself, I think."

"Was that some kind of test?"

"No, no."

"Do they give you orders? Did they make you?"

He kissed me warmly a few times and stroked my hair, pulling on my long curls. "Negrita, mi amor." Then he turned away, looking out the tiny airplane window.

Once home, I was busy working. We had not smuggled anything back, but I was still finishing distributing the last ki Armando had brought back. I had moved all of my product to my new safe house, and sometimes I stopped at Janet's a few times in a day. I passed through her living room greeting the kids, and then went into her bedroom where I locked the door and then opened my tiny safe, exchanging the cash I'd collected for bags of cocaine. Sometimes, I sat on her bed with an electronic scale, a razor, and plastic sandwich bags, packing up the ounces I was about to deliver.

A few days later, I had over ten thousand dollars in my safe and it was only afternoon. So I decided to drop the money off to Armando. I parked near his house, and walked up to the door. Just as I went to push the bell, I noticed his door was not fully closed.

"Estúpido," I muttered to myself, and pushed the door open. The house seemed quiet. My gut filled with fear. What if Armando had been robbed, or arrested, or murdered?

138

I snuck up the stairs quietly, in case there was danger. I took my pepper spray out, trying to prepare. Then, I heard a girl's laughter and my fear turned to rage. I pushed open the bedroom door to see Armando sitting on the edge of his bed, with a girl on her knees before him. His hand rested on her blonde hair and I recognized her as Coco, a fourteen-year old hooker.

He looked up startled to see me there since I had no key.

"Estúpido maricon! Your fucking door was open, pendejo!" I raced down the stairs and he chased after me while trying to button his grey slacks.

"Wait, negrita, wait."

I stood in the living room glaring at him.

"Here," I threw the pile of elastic band bound money at him. "I'm leaving."

"Negrita, please, I love you. I told you, it is only a blow job, it is nothing."

"Shut up, just shut the fuck up! You're nothing but a greasy chulo!" I walked past him heading for the front door. "And you're a fucking idiot! Your door was open, anyone could've walked in."

He grabbed my upper arm and squeezed it tight.

"Let me go, that hurts, cabrón!"

"You do not speak to me like that. Respect!"

"Let go!" I spit at him and he raised his hand as if he was going to hit me.

"Go ahead, hit me, I dare you."

He held his hand high but he did not hit me.

"You don't have the *huevos!*" I screamed.

He let go of me and I ran for the door. I could feel the bruise on my arm throbbing. Coco called out to me, "Wait, chica, please, wait."

"What do you want putania?"

"I'm sorry. Please, girl, believe me, I'm really sorry."

"I bet you are." I walked out the front door and she followed me. I stopped walking and turned to look at her.

"I don't want to do it, I have to. My pimp makes me. He hits me and I have to bring him the coke." She started to cry.

I walked toward her. "Coco, come with me."

"Are you going to hurt me?"

"No, I'm not. *Ven, será fino.* Just come."

We reached my Camaro.

"Get in," I said.

She hesitated, looking frightened.

"Just fucking get in, Coco." I said.

I drove off with her, passing Armando who was standing in the doorway to his house. I took her to my apartment.

"Why are we here?" she asked.

"I'm going to help you."

Once inside, I pulled out a small private stash of coke I kept for friends. "Here's a gram." I handed her a small foil packet.

"A gram?" Her mouth was open in disbelief.

"Why, what was that cabrón giving you?"

"Just a half-gram."

"Look, Coco, I'm going to take you to dinner. You look like a skeleton. Do you ever eat?"

"Not really."

"Here's what we are going to do. You take a nice shower and I'll give you one of my outfits to wear. Then, we'll go have a nice meal and some wine."

She started to cry again. "Why are you being so nice to me?"

"I want to hear your story, that's all." I handed her a bath towel.

While she was in the shower, Armando paged me repeatedly. I opened my apartment door and threw my pager down the stairs. Later, as Coco and I went to dinner, I picked it back up. I had gotten sixteen pages.

I took her to La Casa, where I knew she could drink. I told her to order anything she wanted. Her eyes were huge as she pursued the menu. We drank two bottles of white wine and she told me stories. Her mother died. Her father raped her. She ran away at twelve and her "boyfriend" taught her to turn tricks to support them both. He was now booting cocaine, and so was she. Armando continued to page me through dinner, so I dropped my pager deep into my purse where I could not hear it vibrating.

I went to a pay phone near the ladies room and checked my answering machine remotely. Armando was reminding me in multiple messages that he was flying to Florida later tonight. He was begging me to come by before he left. He said he was so sorry, and that he would never hit me.

After dinner, I asked Coco where she lived.

"The Downtown Hotel."

Of course. This was the hovel where all the hookers in Southbridge lived. I pulled up in front and two girls walked towards the car, thinking I might be a John.

Coco sat in her seat, fresh tears rolling down her face. "I'm just so sorry. You are really nice."

"Chica, stop apologizing. Just forget it. It is not your fault. I want to help you somehow, but I'm not sure what I can do."

"No, I'm okay, really."

I took out my small notebook and wrote my phone number. I handed her the slip of paper. "Here, call me if you ever need to. Please call me."

She hugged me tightly, still sniffling. "Do you forgive me?"

"Of course I do, honey, don't worry."

She got out of the car, and a cluster of girls formed around her. I made a u-turn and drove back uptown. I called Conner from a phone booth.

"Can I come over?"

"Sure, Melissa is here. Stop over and hang out with us."

"Oh, well tell her I said hi." I hung up on him.

Next I called Ryan, but he wasn't home. I looked at my pager. Tyrone had called me a few hours back. I called, but the number just rang. I drove to Armando's and parked far down the street. I waited to see if he went to the airport. While I was waiting, Tyrone paged again. I drove to a phone booth and called him.

"Where are you babygirl? I want to see you."

"Can you come to my apartment around eleven?"

"Okay, where's your man?"

"Away."

"I'll be there."

I went back to Armando's street and spied for over an hour, until I saw Peter come with the limo to get him. He never saw me.

I returned to my apartment where my answering machine's robot voice said, "Message center is full." I hit play and half listened to Armando's messages while I showered. When I got out, I deleted them all. Just before eleven, I got a page from a New York City phone number. I waited ten minutes then called it. A man answered and I asked where I was calling.

"This is a phone booth at JFK."

"I must have dialed wrong," I said.

Tyrone showed up and I led him down the hall to my bedroom. I stripped naked and got into my bed. He followed suit. We kissed for what seemed like hours, and then he tried to fuck me.

"I can't Ty."

"Babygirl, please, are you teasing me?"

"No, I just need you. But look, I can't fuck you and then lie to Armando. You'd want that if you were my boyfriend."

"Will I be your boyfriend?"

"Maybe. Right now, will you just hold me?"

"I will. You know I love you, baby."

I looked at my hand resting on his chest. His ebony coloring was a stark contrast to my pale fingers. He squeezed me tight.

"Tyrone, are you in the mafia?"

He chuckled but didn't answer.

"Where did you get your brand-new Cadillac then? What do you do? I don't even know where you live."

"A girl like you must know not to ask such questions." He kissed my forehead, his soft lips lingering gently. "If you're worried about money, I have plenty to take care of you."

"No, I just don't know anything about you."

"Baby, let's just sleep now."

So we slept. And I clung to him like a life raft. And I didn't cry once.

The next morning, Tyrone kissed me goodbye early, while I was still half-asleep.

"I have to go drive my boss. I'll call you later, beautiful."

I went back to sleep and awoke at noon. I called Armando at home in Florida. After I exchanged hellos with Lourdes through him, he went to a bedroom and closed the door to talk privately with me.

"Negrita, I told you I can do that. I'm a man. I didn't mean for you to see."

How could I tell him much of what disturbed me was her age, which was fourteen? He got Lourdes pregnant at fourteen. I couldn't tell him he was wrong, I was his girlfriend since age sixteen. But I did feel something was wrong with all of it, something I had no words for.

How could I tell him what bothered me most, what haunted me, was Coco's frightened vulnerability, unerasable from her freckled face?

Nineteen

Nine: Slang for a 9-millimeter semiautomatic handgun.

Kickin' Flavor: Starting trouble or acting rowdy.

In the early afternoon, I went to Hector's, then to the Descansar looking for Mateo. I had talked of asking him to be my driver for months, but I also thought I was doing fine without a driver. That day, I finally decided I really needed help.

I found him sitting at the bar, drinking beer while peering at baseball from under a brimmed cap. He was a timorous guy, scrawny and soft-spoken, seemingly poles apart from his rowdy older brother.

"Hey chica!" He kissed my cheek.

"Mateo, can you talk with me?"

"Is everything ok? Armando … is he alright?"

"Everything is fine. I just want to talk some business with you."

We sat at a small table. The bartender promptly delivered a strawberry daiquiri I hadn't ordered.

"Mat, do you have a driver's license?"

"Sure."

"Can I see it?"

He presented his license, and I saw that he was twenty-four. I was surprised because with his weathered face, I thought he was more like thirty.

"How would you like to work for me as my driver?"

"Really? Seriously?"

"Yes, as long as you're a good driver and you don't break any traffic rules. Not even one."

"Oh, I'm a really good driver."

"Great, how many beers have you had?"

"Just this one."

I took out a twenty-dollar bill and placed it on the table along with my keys. "Then let's go. Take me for a ride," I said.

As we walked toward my car, which was parked along the curb in front of the bar, Tyrone pulled up. He rolled down the car window and motioned me to come over.

"Babygirl, come're."

"I can't."

"I just need to tell you something."

I looked over at Mateo. He was busy starting my car. I took a step into the street towards Tyrone's white Cadillac. He reached his arm out the window, grabbing the lapel of my leather jacket and pulling me towards him. He gave me a firm kiss me on the lips.

I stepped back. "Jerk!"

"I'll call you later, love." He drove off.

I turned around to see Carlos standing on the sidewalk near my car.

"Kicking flavor!" he called to me. Then he began talking to his brother through my car's window.

My heart froze. This ridiculously small town seemed to contain about five streets in total. I got in the passenger seat and leaned over to talk to Carlos out the driver's window.

"We gotta go, Carlos. We'll be back in a few."

I was scared, but I told myself it would be cool even if he told Armando about Tyrone. I kissed my friends. Plus, Armando would only ask if I fucked Ty and I could easily answer no.

Mateo drove off. We drove around town as I explained the job to him. He'd have to swear secrecy, which would be easy because he was fiercely loyal to Armando. In fact, I think Armando had him on the dole. I explained to him that if we were pulled over, the cops could search him and even the car, but not me or my purse. This is what a crooked cop told Armando. He said that passengers could not be searched without a warrant.

"This way," I said, "I can't be searched and all the drugs will be in my purse or on my body."

"I really want to do it," he said.

"Cool! On the days you drive me you can't be drunk. You can't drink until we are done. It is just a few days a week or less, but sometimes when I get a shipment we might be in the car ten straight hours doing deliveries. I'll get you a pager. When I call you, you call me back and I'll tell you the days and times."

"Do I come to your apartment?"

"No, I'll come get you. We start each shift at my safe house. There's a small strip of stores just around the corner from it so you'll park there and I'll walk to the house. In general, you'll park around the corner from where I'm going."

"Thank you, gracias. It all sounds so cool."

"Great. Now take me to your apartment so I know where you live."

He took me to a drab, almost empty studio apartment.

Then I had a scary thought.

"Is Carlos staying here with you?" I asked.

"Oh no, he can't. I'm on probation."

"Probation?"

"Yeah, just some trouble I got in with my ex, fucking puta. It's cool. I'm a good boy now. I always see my officer when I'm supposed to. I can't associate with any convicted felons though, not even my own brother."

My stomach dropped, churning with unease. He must have beaten her, that was the only thing I could think of. He asked me if I wanted to go back to the bar. I said yes because when I was twelve, I learned that alcohol drowns the voice of fear. (It also stops crying that won't cease, and brings that ever-elusive sleep.) So I had to go, because I seriously needed a drink.

The evenings were turning crisp. I was now wearing my much loved, full-length white sweater with brown wooden buttons. I drove around town in my Camaro, picking up Colleen, then Seely, and then a new friend I met at the disco named Nikki. Seely's boyfriend Mike reminded me he was coming to pick her up at the Disco Lounge at 11 p.m. He wasn't fond of me dropping her off at 5 a.m., when I normally rolled home.

It was a girl's night out, the kind I usually hosted a few nights each week while Armando was in Florida. The itinerary never changed. There was dinner at La Casa, followed by drinking and dancing at The Disco Lounge. More and more of my friends were showing up regularly at The Lounge. And Conner was always there, faithfully working security at the door, Sherry was behind the bar, and Tommy lived in the DJ booth. Tyrone was sometimes hanging around, and Ryan too. Colleen or Seely were often on the dance floor with me. I out-danced everyone.

I would toss my heels into the DJ booth and dance in my stockings for hours, only pausing to chug my drink or do a few shots.

Tommy grabbed my arm as I raced into the booth. "Girlfriend, will you turn me on?"

"Sure baby." I tossed him my kit.

"And will you DJ while I go?"

"Woo-hoo! Fuck yeah."

It was a thrill for me to spin. Tommy had taught me to work the lights, then later the turntables.

"Whatcha gonna play?" he asked.

"Um, okay, "Friends," definitely, oh, and "Lovergirl," the twelve inch. If you're still not back, um, let's see … I got it, "In My House.""

"You go, girl!" he said.

I was dancing in the booth with headphones on singing along with Teena Marie. The lyrics were sexy. I felt Tommy's arms close around my waist and his entire body press against mine. We danced like this, while I cued up my next song, then he sat on his stool and pulled me onto his lap, as he often did.

"Girl, I got serious problems with Mark."

"Why, what's wrong?" Mark was Tommy's live-in boyfriend.

"He is insanely jealous of you."

"Me? Why the fuck me? You're gay."

"I know, he's just a bitch, you know how he is. He knows you take me to New York City and we buy records together. He knows you give me blow. He's jealous of how much we hang out."

"Well why the fuck doesn't he come out? He can dance with me all night. We'll all hang. I'll turn him on too."

"He's all mad at me for doing so much blow. And he thinks you're evil for giving it to me."

We both cracked up laughing.

"Stop it, don't make me laugh," he said. "This is serious, he's driving me nuts, nagging me constantly."

"So ditch the bitch." I started playing with the board, making the colored lights over the dance floor flicker.

"I love him."

"Yeah, I know." I jumped off his lap, kissing his cheek. "I gotta dance to this."

"Can I come to your house?"

"No! Do you want to make it worse?"

"I just don't want to go home."

"We'll decide later. I love you." I wriggled onto the crowded dance floor, and danced and danced until I was no longer thinking.

Later, I got a table with the girls, and we sat at it drinking shots of schnapps. I could see the door from my seat and I saw Carlos walk in. He smiled big at me and waved.

"Oh, mierda, chulo cabrón," I said under my breath. All the girls looked at me questioningly.

He walked up to our table. "Chica, cómo estás?" He took my hand and kissed it.

"Bien."

"Who are all these lovely ladies?" he asked.

I introduced him to my sister and friends, and he kissed each girl's hand. He wore a black felt hat with small feathers tucked into the band, and a white satin jacket with matching satin pants. He looked creepy as well as crazy.

"So, chica," he said, "did you hear the racket around the block from your house?"

"No."

"Oh, it was so funny. I had my boy drive me slow up Mill Street, where I hung out the window with a shotgun and blew out all the windshields of the parked cars. Then, I drove back through and tossed handfuls of twenty-dollar bills out the window. People were running everywhere. It was hilarious!"

"Holy shit, did the cops come?" Colleen asked.

"Yeah, after about an hour. By then we ditched the car, and I was just one of the crowd." He howled with laughter at his own joke. "I was kickin' flavor! Everyone's gonna know I'm boss of this town."

He walked away and we all looked at each other with dread.

I got up and walked towards the bar. Conner stopped me. We talked in a corner about his next order, and he asked me about Nikki.

"She's so sexy, right?" I said.

"Yeah, but why do you say that?"

"Because her and I talked about having a threesome with you." I walked away, reveling in my brazenness.

Carlos was suddenly standing before me among the crowd. "Hey, putania, I know you mess around on my brother-in-law."

"That's bullshit, and don't call me a whore, bastardo."

He grabbed my sleeve, "Mira, I watch out for his interests."

I pulled my arm away. "Let go of me!"

"Whadda you gonna do, tell him I know about you?"

"You know nothing, stupid maricón."

I pushed past him towards the bar then stood behind it with my arm around Sherry. She eventually made me a daiquiri. After I finished it, I went and grabbed the girls. I led them all to the ladies' room, where I held court in the lounge.

"Sissy, who is that Carlos guy?" Seely said. She was sitting on top of the vanity while the triple mirrors behind her reflected dark hair spilling down her back.

"No one you ever want to know. Do not ever drink or dance with him, just stay away, he's totally insane," I said.

Seely went home, and as it got later Colleen left too, grabbing a ride from a guy she knew and citing her boyfriend's expected early morning arrival.

I walked around the thinning bar crowd holding hands with Nikki. She was tall and slender, with a shiny auburn mane. She wore thick raccoon eyeliner that made her look like a rock star. I met her randomly one night, and we clicked right away. I instantly made her a member of my posse.

Nikki and I went and flirted with Conner. We walked away laughing when he was dumbstruck by our suggestion he take us for a ride in his new car.

As the bar was closing, Tommy invited Nikki and me to an after-hours party. It was taking place at a house next door to the club. We decided to go, and we ended up in the basement apartment of some guy we had never met. About eight of us sat around the coffee table on the floor, passing around a large mirror with lines of coke on top.

The sun came into the window announcing dawn. We were still busy passing the mirror.

There was hard rapping on the door. Everyone grew silent and paranoid. The mirror was hastily pushed underneath the couch. The guy who lived in the apartment came back with Armando and a man I never saw before. Sherry, Tommy, and Rob called out their hellos to Armando. He came around to where I was and sat on the floor next to me.

"Negrita, I'm back." He gave me a passionate kiss. "Are you being good?"

"Sí,"

"Good. This is my amigo, Rafa."

"Como estás," I said. He smiled and shook his head.

Armando was extremely drunk. "Negrita, I came to find you. I told my friend, 'I'm gonna find this bitch kissing on some other guy and I'm gonna beat her.'" He giggled, but everyone else was quiet.

152

"Come on, she's my girlfriend," he said to no one in particular. He took out an eight-ball of coke and threw it on the table. "There, everyone salud, *celebremos!*"

Jonesing fingers ripped the plastic bag off the coke, and went back to the task of cutting lines with a blade. Armando kept kissing me and squeezing me tightly.

"Cabrón, stop." I pushed him away.

"Negrita, you never push me." He put his hand on my back and grabbed hold of my hair. Then he pulled on it, hard. No one could see.

I rubbed his other arm and smiled, and he slowly let go of me. When he got up to go to the bathroom I leaned over to whisper to Tommy.

"You can't stay over tonight, baby, I'm sorry."

"No problem," he said, barely making eye contact with me.

A few weeks later, I uncovered a plot against me. Two guys of my acquaintance were going to rob me at gunpoint; at least that's what Ryan swore he heard. He said they plotted in front of him and made him promise not to tell anyone. They had no idea how close we were. He said they were going to try to get into my apartment by invitation to case the place, and then come rob me in ski masks.

When he told me I wasn't convinced they were serious, but then one of the guys started calling me out of the blue, asking to come over to my apartment and make me dinner, saying he was a chef. It was weird. We weren't close friends and he had a girlfriend. He didn't mention her in these dinner plans. I put him off politely, but he called repeatedly, as if him making me dinner was urgent.

I asked Armando's advice and he told me to sic Carlos on them.

"*Es loco!*" I said.

"No, he is family, he will help you. Call him. We need a bouncer anyway. I cannot go, you know that."

I called him, and Carlos agreed to scare the guys. I picked him up at his apartment one evening, and then I called the chef. I told him I was in his hood and I thought I'd drop by. He told me to come over.

I knocked on his door and when he opened it, I asked him to come outside. He stepped out onto the sidewalk in his socks.

"What's up?"

"Hello," said Carlos, stepping out of the shadows.

He was pointing a nine at the chef. Then, he jabbed the gun into his side. I stood stunned. I had no idea Carlos was packing. This was not what I asked him to do.

The chef looked at me with rage, while keeping his hands slightly up.

"Listen up, gringo, she is my boy's lady. And you better never mess with her," Carlos said.

"I wouldn't, I don't know what this is about." He looked at me, terrified. "What's up, what is this about?" he said.

"Chica, don't answer this pendejo," Carlos said. "You, motherfucker, don't even be talking to her. You're not making her dinner or her man is gonna send me here to kill you. I know where you live so just stay the fuck away from her."

"I got it, I swear," the chef said, his eyes still glued on me. They were brimming with hatred.

When we got to the car Carlos roared with laughter, retelling the story over and over as if I wasn't right there when it happened.

"Kickin' flavor! Now chica, take me for a drink." He pulled the seat release so the seat slid all the way back and he plopped his sneakered feet on top of the dashboard.

We went to Hector's. I ordered single malt scotch on the rocks. I drank the hard liquor like medicine, hoping it would seep in and stop the quaking in my bones.

154

"Aren't you afraid of getting in trouble again, Carlos, you know, of going back to prison?"

"Hell no! I was born and raised in prison, and I plan to die there too. I can't wait to get back."

"But why?"

"Order, chica, you know, routine. Got my room, three squares, my boys. I get up in the morning when the bell rings, eat when the bell rings, go to sleep when the bell rings. I don't have to think. I hate it out here, it's too crazy for me."

Twenty

Mule: A person hired by a dealer to smuggle or carry illegal drugs from one destination to another.

Swaying slightly on her feet, Colleen walked over to me on the dance floor. Clearly smashed, she gave me a hard shove.

"Tu madre es puta," she said.

"Get away, perra." I said, pushing her back.

She grabbed my hair, and we began one of our now infamous bitch fights. These spontaneous brawls were now an expected eventuality, especially if either of us was more drunk than usual.

As we struggled I tripped her and she tumbled down, grabbing my arm and pulling me to the floor with her. We laughed, squealing like schoolgirls, and we cursed like sailors—though all in Spanish.

"*Tú eres una concha … a mierda!*" I yelled at her while pulling free from her grasp. We were now sitting on the dance floor with an uneasy crowd watching.

"*Besa mi concha*, perra," she said, attempting to smack me but missing. "Tu madre es puta!"

"No, tu madre es puta!" I said.

Armando had taught us this, telling us it meant, "your mother's a whore." We adopted it, at first repeating it for fun. But somehow we ended up chanting to each other like a jump rope song when we got drunk, and it always led to brawling.

I felt Conner's arms reaching under mine, picking me up and pulling me away. Another bouncer grabbed Colleen. As we were escorted to the front of the bar we continued yelling insults in faltering Spanish at each other. We were brought to stools at the bar. We sat down on them next to each other as if nothing was wrong.

"Sherry, give us shots!" I said.

Conner protested. "No drinks, you girls got to chill. You're both drinking too much, and you can't be scrapping on the dance floor."

"Fuck you, Conner, you don't tell me what to do, get away from me!"

I looked at Colleen and we burst into hysterics. He frowned, sighing in frustration, but as he walked away he gave Sherry the okay nod. In no time, Colleen and I were tossing back shots.

"He's such a pussy," I said.

"Speaking of pussy, where's your little perra tonight?"

"Why you gotta hate Nikki so much Coll? She's cool."

"You blow me off for her. Besides, she's all quiet and boring."

"I don't! You just can't always come out. You have Estéban. I still fucking love you the same, girl, and Nikki isn't boring. She's deep."

"You mean she's weird, like you loco bitch!"

It was true. I liked being with Nikki more than Colleen. I couldn't help it. Nikki was docile and lacking the mean streak Colleen often

158

smarted me with. Her stalwart eyes were placid, and she had a smoldering sexuality and an ethnic look that attracted me.

Nikki slept many nights at my house with me in my bed. It was not unusual. It was what friends did. But there was an added element of intimacy I had not felt with any of my other girlfriends. We often stayed up all night snuggled close together, talking in the dark. On many of those nights, I was secretly sure I was in love with her.

She had turned tricks before and though she wasn't currently hooking, she spoke in a sexually frank way I'd only heard hookers do. Soon we were swapping stories from our sex lives. We shared how we always wanted to do a threesome. I suggested we work on Conner and Ryan, but not Armando. He clung to the fantasy that I was far more innocent then I was, so I hid both my predilections and my past experiences from him. I also didn't want to risk him being jealous of my girlfriends. I spent most of my time with them.

In order to help Nikki out with money, and to bring her closer, I asked Armando if he might make her a smuggler.

"Are you sure we can trust her?"

"Yes, I know her so well, even though it has not been long. She is totally cool. She lives with her mother, she doesn't even have a boyfriend."

"Bien, then we will all go to Florida together."

"That's it, you want her to do it?"

"She can try it. If it works, she is *perfecta, maravillosa*. No one will mess with her. Federales will flirt with her while she holds a suitcase full of coke she is so *hermosa*."

"Yeah, she is beautiful, but mira, this is work. She is not for you to fuck." "Yes negrita, but me, I would love to *tener sexo con* … yes, I like her mucho."

"Just shut the fuck up, maricón!" I said.

He flashed me that winning grin that always forced me to smile in return.

Two weeks later, in a rented Lincoln Towncar, the three of us headed to Miami. Armando and I split the driving, and we were there in twenty-four hours flat. We stayed at the Hyatt in Miami again. Armando was away most of the day. Nikki and I lived at the pool where we drank all day, starting with mimosas at breakfast and ending the day with white wine.

Each night we went to a fancy restaurant. Nikki and I would dress up like sexy teen sluts with big hair, bright blue eye shadow, dark red lips, mini-skirts, and shiny vinyl belts with matching shoes. We also wore black lace gloves, dozens of bracelets, and huge, garish crosses like our fashion idol, Madonna.

Armando invited various men to dinner with us each night, none of whom spoke English. Nikki and I sat close together, preening and having a private conversation. The men were agog. They could not stop staring at us during dinner, which was our intention. We giggled at their drooling. Armando would brag to them about his "mujeres gringas." Twice, he convinced me to take an order to the bar, and then return with the drinks and serve the men while they clapped and chortled. Armando would then pull me onto his lap, nuzzling me and grabbing my ass as if to show them I was his cute trick pony.

Nikki became our mule. Armando went, as always, to make the buy and visit his family, only now he no longer carried the kilos back on the plane. Nikki flew there and back in one day, using ticket reservations in fake names.

Back home, Nikki and I plotted to seduce Ryan. We even planned to go all the way, something I had not done since I had become Armando's

160

girlfriend. We shopped for matching lingerie at the mall, then stopped and grabbed some peach schnapps. We drank straight from the bottle while we dressed each other up in push-up bras, garter belts, stockings and heels. Our idea of sexy clothes came entirely from a Fredrick's Of Hollywood catalogue.

We paged Ryan and convinced him to come to my apartment, telling him we were bored and we wanted him to come party with us. When we opened the door in red satin and black lace, he started stepping backwards down the narrow stairs that led to my door.

"Come on, Ryan," I said.

Nikki stood behind me and dropped her head on my shoulder, giving him a seductive stare.

"You two are fucking nuts, come on, your man will cut my thing off!"

"He's in Florida."

"How do you know for sure?"

"Because I know. I just called there, like, two hours ago," I said.

"Yeah, so he could be here in three."

"Ryan, just come inside!" Nikki said.

We both grabbed him and pulled him in by his jacket. He sat on my couch like a captured animal, looking terrified and taking long swills from the bottle of schnapps. Nikki and I left him to roll a joint. We walked down the hall to my bedroom holding hands.

"Fuck it girlfriend, he's right, Armando would kill him. Plus, he probably won't be able to get it up, he's too scared, and not just of your man," Nikki said.

We laughed, covering our mouths so he wouldn't hear us.

"He's fucking sexy though, Nik, and he's so stoic he'd never tell anyone."

"How old is he?" she asked.

"He's, like, nineteen."

"Let's get a man, he won't be scared."

"Yeah, but a man will brag and I know Ryan won't."

We returned to the living room, sitting on each side of him. We got him to make-out with us in turn, but we could not get him to do more no matter we each pulled every trick we knew.

Nikki and I practically dragged that boy to my bedroom and then pleaded discomfort with the corsets and nylon, stripping naked in front of him, but he turned his face away. As we went to sleep, he refused to get into my bed with us. Instead, he sat in a small gold velvet antique chair in the corner of my bedroom and slept with one eye open, swearing to us he was going out the window and down the fire escape if Armando showed up.

I was now making my rounds with Mateo as my driver and I loved it. I never liked driving, plus I felt safer. I also loved hiring people.

One cold afternoon, Mateo parked near a corner and I jumped out of the car, heading for the Lincoln brothers' house.

"Babygirl! We've been missing you so much. You never visit!" Jamal hugged me tightly at the door.

"Hey, I come when you call," I said.

"'Cause you always chasing the dollar."

"Yo, bitch, I gotta survive."

"I know, I know. Here, sit with me," he said.

I sat on his lap. I had not seen him for a few weeks and he now had a dry, hacking cough.

"What's up with you, Jamal?"

"I don't know girl, I got this flu shit that is not getting better. I feel like crap."

"Did you go to the doctor?"

"Free clinic. Doc gave me antibiotics and I got a little better."

I hugged him tightly. "You'll be okay."

"Yes I will, this daddy is gonna be fine."

We went to his bedroom, where I grabbed a black silky feather boa and wrapped it around my neck before plopping on the bed. Jamal sat next to me and started laying out piles of cash. He looked a bit weary.

"Jam, why don't you put on blue eye-shadow? That always makes you look cute."

"Okay, gimme your makeup case. I like the blue you got on now."

I tossed my padded cosmetic bag to him. While I counted the money, he sat in front of his dresser looking into a table mirror, putting on my mascara.

Armando was away and I was dancing into my third hour at The Lounge. Tommy was sulking because Mark had told him not to come home. I danced over to the booth and Tommy and I each held each other around the waist with both arms.

"Lover, you gotta let me sleep at your place. I was up all night fighting. I need some rest. I'm gonna cut out early, nobody comes out on Tuesday anyway."

"Okay, Tommy, sure."

At 1:00 a.m. Tommy drove me home in my Camaro. He half carried me up the three flights of stairs to my apartment because I was so drunk, which made me wonder how I got home alone so many nights. I always called my friends when I awoke in bed with no memory of the end part of the past night. They'd always tell me despite their protests, I'd drive myself home, insisting I was fine. Sometimes they said I had tossed chairs and tables around to support my argument.

In my apartment, I gave Tommy some lines and we drank scotch, since it was all I had. I put on a short nightgown, not thinking of Tommy as a man, but more as one of my girlfriends. Even Armando would be cool if he was here. We got into bed and I placed my head on his chest.

He lifted my chin up and kissed me. Then, he kept on kissing me.

"Wait, stop … I thought you are gay," I said.

"I am. It's just kissing."

"I thought gay guys don't kiss girls."

"Well, I want to kiss you. No one will know."

So we made out. Not because I was attracted to him but because I loved him, he was one of my best friends, and because kissing a gay man was strange and daring.

I paid for my indiscretion shortly after, when Mark began regularly leaving ranting messages on my machine. Drunk and hysterical, he would scream, "Witch!" between rambling accusations of me man-stealing and making Tommy a Joneser. Tommy swore he told Mark nothing but Mark harassed me for weeks, sometimes calling ten times in a night.

Finally, I had to tell Armando, who had just returned from fourteen days in Colombia.

He was leaning against the wall at the Lounge, holding a scotch and schmoozing with people sitting at the table. I went up to him and pressed myself into the nook of his arm. When he turned his attention to me, I told him about the messages.

"*Qué niño estúpido*," said Armando. "Tommy is so gay. He does not like women. Everyone knows that. He's cómo se dice? … *como una mujer?*"

"I think you mean feminine," I said. It was true Tommy had effeminate gestures. People knew he was gay within a minute of meeting him.

"Mark must stop phoning you, you don't need that mierda. I will speak to Tommy."

164

"Okay, negrita," I said. I kissed him and smiled. "Just be bueno, eh? Tommy's my best friend."

"Sí, sí, negrita." He pulled me closer and tighter, his breathing got more urgent. We decided to leave the club early, right after he talked to Tommy.

Back at my house we rolled in the sheets, declaring our love and allegiance to each other. We slept tangled together, as we always did. I hated to admit it, even to myself, but I felt safer when he was with me. And I had grown to adore him more than I ever thought I could. I had always found his looks heart stopping, but when I saw him asleep he looked almost angelic. Over the years he remained enigmatic and reticent, but I had seen sides of him that were naïve, even incorrupt. They induced me to love him more than I ever should have.

Twenty-One

Christmas season, and Armando and I were dressed to the nines practically every night. We attended big parties everywhere; at the Lincoln brothers', at Conner's, and at The Disco Lounge, where we were the only non-staff invited.

Those friends whose parties we graced treated us like saints who had given them a benediction. I believed it was because people knew that over the past few months, Armando had developed the habit of throwing down eight-balls as party favors. When we arrived at parties, we were ushered in with deference, immediately attended to, and quickly invited to the 'back room'. We didn't do drugs, but we gave them out.

Once, I told Armando over dinner that I was worried we were making the whole town into junkies. Even Seely was stumbling trying to stay off it.

"Negrita," he said, "I thought you believed in, ah, *legalización* of all drugs."

"I do. It's just, well, Gregg actually booted up in my living room the other day. It was so gross. I went to see his madre, and she cried to me, 'My son's a junkie!'"

I had known Gregg since we were thirteen. I always called him Gregg Allman for his resemblance to the striking singer. Gregg was a bad boy who came from one of the toughest, most racially divided neighborhoods of Southbridge.

"Some people cannot handle any things, sí? That is not our problema, chica."

I didn't bother to remind him that I likely supplied Gregg's dealer's dealer, since we were practically supplying the entire town. When we first started, I was wracked inside with guilt and confusion. But over time those feelings dimmed, and my attention became fixed on alcohol, illicit sex, money, and glittering gold jewelry.

A few days before Christmas, there was a public bash at The Lounge. We hired Peter to take us in the limo, and I had him pick up my girls: Seely, Colleen and Nikki. Armando loved arriving with four pretty girls. He kept mentioning his white girl harem fantasies to us.

We girls drank and danced all night, and we sat at times in the ladies room lounge, snorting coke off of the counter. I only did one line, but I let everyone else do as much as they wanted, even Seely, though I told her it was only because it was Christmas.

Armando could be found as usual in a corner, chatting up some girl, or at the bar, buying drinks for everyone.

It was a magical night, and the future looked sparkling. Then Carlos showed up and Armando declared we all get a table and sit together. He ordered Champagne. Carlos was wearing a red velvet sweat suit with a Santa hat, and regaling us with tales of his latest exploits.

"Yeah, I'm housin' a pit now. Trying to toughen him up. I fed him some of those nice white bunny rabbits I got at the pet store."

All the girls protested and admonished him at once, sounding like a flock of birds. He looked around the table, his grin expanding. He loved the attention of upsetting everyone.

"Man, Armando, these perras are tough."

"Vete pa' carajo, estúpido maricón! Don't call us that!" I said.

"Perdóneme, señorita," he said, placing his hand on his heart in an exaggerated gesture, "Armando can't you put a leash on her?"

"Carlos, silcencio!" said Armando.

He then admonished Carlos in rapid Spanish, temporarily shutting him up.

"Something very strange happened to me," Armando said, "I was walking down the street, and I saw a man take a picture of me from across the street. When I went towards him, he kept taking pictures. Then he ran off."

"Did you chase him?" I asked.

"No, no. There was ice, and my shoes were, uh … como se dice, resbaladizo?" He put his hand on my arm to wait for my translation.

"I don't know, smooth? Slippery?"

"Sí, sí."

"Who do you think it was?" asked Seely, her eyes wide.

"The cops, it has to be the pigs … quién más, negrita?

"Well, it is posible you have made enemies," I said, thinking maybe some people were jealous of his success.

"It was the federales, I am sure. Ah, but they will never touch me, I am invincible!"

He raised his champagne glass, smiling, and everyone else did too. Except for Carlos, who kept his head down the table like a sullen kid and only briefly lifted his eyes to meet mine.

That night at Armando's house, in bed, I laid my cheek on his bare chest while he encircled me with his arms.

"Mi amor," I said, "I am afraid of Carlos, very afraid. Can't we send him to live in Miami? Or maybe even New York City?"

"I cannot. I would have to set him up and he'd blow *todo el dinero,* and then be back in a week."

"But he said he wants to go back to prison, and that he can't wait to get there. What if he takes us with him?"

"No *te preocupes.* I will protect you, negrita, I swear to you—he fears me."

But I thought of Carlos' defiance during Armando's toast to invincibility. I could see his mutinous eyes in my mind.

Armando flew to Key Biscayne for Christmas, but he was back a week later. I was dressing for a night of partying with Colleen when he called and said he was home. We agreed to meet at The Disco Lounge later that night. He told me he had a surprise for me. It turned out to be Lourdes. She had returned with him for a New Year's Eve out, and to see her brothers.

"Lourdes, cómo estás?"

I kissed her plump cheeks. Her brown skin looked radiant with sun, and her shiny dark hair was as long as ever. She was draped in gold jewelry, and wearing a fur wrap over an expensive designer dress.

"I am so excited to be here!" she said. "Did Armando tell you I want to go shopping with you?"

"No, he didn't, but I'd love that."

People were confused all night, but since it was New Year's they were so fucked up it didn't matter. Everyone thought of Armando and me as a couple, and we didn't tell them about Lourdes or about Florida. It wasn't a strict secret, we just never told our business. Plus, it helped keep her and José safe. All night I fielded reports of him cheating on me. I'd answer nonchalantly, "Oh, no he's not, that's his wife." Not one person questioned me further.

Lourdes and I danced together for hours. Of course, my close friends knew all about her. Nikki was neutral as always. Seely loved her and danced with her too, but Colleen was angry.

"Why do you want to hang out with his wife?"

"Because she's fun and I like her. She's got his kid, but I'm his girlfriend. It's cool."

"Bitch, you're a fucking wack job," Colleen said.

"Go fuck yourself, you're just jealous. And listen, I promised Armando we would not fight tonight, so I'm outta here." I pushed past her and walked away.

Two days later, I went shopping with Lourdes. We strapped a car seat into my Camaro, and Armando kissed us both goodbye. I drove us to New Jersey, where we shopped at Saks Fifth Avenue.

"We don't have these malls on the key," she said.

We shopped for José, buying him clothes and shoes, and we bought ourselves gold earrings, shoes, clothes, scarves, sweaters, and we got a few things for Armando. My entire trunk was stuffed with our booty.

Hungry from shopping, we went to a steakhouse.

Lourdes said, "You know, I feel happy Armando has you. I worried about who he will go with, you know, girls, but I know he is okay with you. I trust you."

"Thank you, girlfriend, you are so sweet to me."

I smiled at her, and I decided not to tell her that her husband cheats on us with coke whores.

Twenty-Two

On The Cuff: Items (such as drugs) given to a person without him paying for them, with the promise of future payment. To give something on credit.

"Armando, do you think you will always be with Lourdes?"

I asked the question one night out of nowhere, but I had wondered it since I first became his girlfriend.

"Sí, sí, always I will be. She has my son."

He leaned over our dinner plates and kissed me.

"Well, what about me, will you always be with me? What do you think about our future?"

"Babe, we ain't got no future," he said plainly, taking a deep drink of his wine.

I was afraid. I'd never seen anything end well, and I had witnessed three divorces among my parents. There was tandem screaming,

overturned dinner tables, slapping and hitting—including us kids—
and finally, state troopers sitting on the couch with squawking radios
on their belts.

If Armando and I had no future, how would it end?

A few weeks later, Colleen and I were dressing at my apartment for a
night out. We were having dinner together, and then meeting Armando
at The Disco Lounge.

Once there, I had trouble finding Armando. His car was in the
parking lot so I knew he was there. Walking through the crowd slowly, I
finally spotted him in a dark corner. Ignoring the room, he stood close
to a girl, leaning his arm against the wall beside her. I went over and
tugged the back of his long wool coat. He turned around, a look of
annoyance quickly turning to a look of fear.

"Ay! Negrita, so you are here."

"Yes, I am."

"Mira, you must meet Lisa."

"Hello," I said, while I shot Armando an angry look. There was an
awkward silence. "Well, see you later," I said, then stalked off. He didn't
follow me.

I sat at the bar, furious, drinking shots, until Tommy begged me to
come and dance. I turned him on in the DJ booth, and then danced for
a while. Colleen flitted on and off the floor. But thoughts of Armando
were nagging me so I went again in search of him. He was now standing
arm in arm with this woman.

"*Qué está pasando*? Estúpido maricón!" I said.

"I'm not doing nothing, negrita, I swear. She is a lesbian. Lisa, tell
her." He was laughing hysterically, and I realized he was drunk.

Lisa, a tall, blonde woman in her twenties, was stunningly beautiful.
She glowed with the flush of newfound intrigue. I felt like a little kid

compared to her. Looking down at me, smiling broadly while holding my man's arm, she laughingly agreed, "Yeah, it's true, I'm a lesbian."

"You *lesbiana*? That's bullshit! You're both liars."

They laughed as if we were playing a silly game. I walked away and went back to the dance floor, dancing for hours in my stocking feet, escaping into the music, only stopping to drink the shots Sherry kept sending me from the bar.

Later, I went for the third time that night to find my boyfriend. The bastard never came to see me once. Now, he was nowhere to be found. I went into the parking lot in my stockings, though Conner tried to stop me. I was sure I would bust them in the car. I picked up a rock, ready to smash the window, but Armando's car was gone.

The Disco Lounge closed, and I stayed with a small crowd including Colleen, who was sleeping at my house. I drank nonstop while laying out lines of coke on top of the bar for everyone there. I called Armando every name I could think of to whoever would listen. I felt totally humiliated. Everyone knew he ditched me and left the bar with some girl.

It was past 6 a.m. I told Colleen I was sure Armando was home and I was going there.

"Come on, fuck him. He's an asshole, let's just go home," she said.

"No! I'm going to confront them at his house."

We got in the car and I drove fast, pouring my anger through my pedal-pushing foot.

"Slow down, *puta*," Colleen screamed at me.

"Fuck you perra, it's not your man fucking a whore somewhere!"

She punched me in the arm and I slapped her back. We continued to scrap while I drove the car.

The fighting was making me swerve. I double parked in front of Armando's door, but I could see he wasn't there. I then drove all over town looking for him, while Colleen continued to protest. I went into all the bars I knew had after-hours, and then I went to the Downtown Hotel, but Armando, and his red IROC-Z, were nowhere to be found. Finally, I concluded he was at Lisa's house, and I had no idea where that was since I'd never seen the bitch before tonight.

I drove to my apartment, defeated. Colleen pulled out the couch bed and lay down exhausted. I walked down the long hall to my bedroom to get her pillows. When I gave them to her, I took the cordless phone off the base. Colleen looked at me with disgust.

"Now you're gonna wait for that cabrón to call you?"

"Just go to sleep, bitch," I said, kissing her on top of the head.

I fell into a troubled sleep. At 9:00 a.m., my phone rang.

"Fucking pendejo," I screamed into the phone.

"Negrita, you cannot answer the phone this way."

"I can do whatever the fuck I want, just like you!" I hung up on him. He immediately called back.

"Negrita, let me come over."

"Go take a shower, motherfucker!" I said, and then I hung up on him again.

He called back, trying to explain.

"I was just at Hector's."

"No you weren't, you lying cabrón! I went there!"

"You must have missed me. I need to sleep; you know I hate to sleep alone. Let me come there."

"Fuck off!!"

At that point, Colleen bust through my bedroom door and grabbed the phone, screaming into it, "Stop calling here, we're asleep!" She hung it up and threw it at me, hard. I chased her down the hall and we

176

fought, punching each other, while my phone rang incessantly. She ran to the base and unplugged it from the wall. I grabbed it away and took it to my bedroom, where there was another jack.

She called down the hall, "You're a perra, and tu madre es puta!"

I slammed my bedroom door and pushed the slide lock, then plugged the phone in and commenced screaming at Armando and hanging up on him. Colleen returned and tried to break my door down.

"Negrita, *por favor*, I have to leave for Miami tonight, I must see you."

"Pendejo, we are through. Do you *comprende*? You are not my boyfriend, you are nothing!" I slammed the phone down and fell into a deep sleep. When I awoke that evening, it was dark. Colleen and I had terrible hangovers. We went to a diner and ate breakfast at 6 p.m., neither of us talking about the morning.

Armando stayed in Florida for almost two weeks. He called daily, but I never picked up or called him back, until he left a message saying we had to talk business.

"Negrita, I missed you so much."

"That's not business. Talk business or I'm hanging up."

"I need you to go see Carlos, bring him three, on the cuff."

"Sí. Goodbye."

"No! Wait … I must tell you … I love you."

"Okay, goodbye."

"Mira, listen to me, I did not have sex with Lisa, I swear on my Saint Christopher!"

"I guess nothing is sacred to you, then."

"Qué?"

"Nothing, bye." I hung up and he called back, but I didn't answer.

I escaped the pain of my perceived loss with twice as much drinking. I fooled around with Tyrone and Ryan. Tyrone engaged me in the usual tug of war over whether or not I would now become his girlfriend.

I went to Carlos's apartment one day, already slightly drunk. When I knocked he called out, "Come in."

I went inside but did not see him.

"I'm in here, putaña," he called from the bathroom.

I tentatively walked towards the door.

"Come in, don't be shy." He was in a deep claw foot tub with his back to me. I walked in and closed the lid of the toilet and sat on it, facing him.

"Girlfriend, why you been crying?"

"Armando and I broke up."

"So why not get comfort from one of your boys?"

"What are you talking about, pendejo?"

He laughed. "I got eyes, puta, eyes and ears. Got them in prison."

"You're psychotic."

"Come into the bath with me."

"No way!"

"Come on, this tub is big, you'll feel better. I'll wash your back."

"No thanks."

"Putaña! You do not want Armando to know what you do when he is away, plus I don't like pussy. Have you ever seen me with a bitch?"

"Actually, no."

"That's right! Girls are nasty. You know, when I first went to prison, when I was fourteen, I was held down and raped. But by the time I was sixteen, I was the one doing the raping. Ha-ha! Kickin' flavor! Now, I like boys."

I pulled a flask of schnapps out of my purse and drank deeply from it.

"Come on, putaña, I won't bite. I swear."

For reasons I cannot say, because I don't know what they are and likely never will, I peeled my clothes off and got into the tub with him.

He began to wash my back as promised and I started to sob.

"There, there, partner, it's okay." He put his arms around my front and I started to squirm. Crossing them over my chest he grabbed onto each shoulder and held me sitting where I was. Then, he started penetrating me.

"No, stop!" I pushed on his arms, trying to get free.

"Come on, partner, you'll feel better."

"Stop calling me partner, maricón!"

I continued to struggle but I could not free myself from his tight grip. "Ouch, come on motherfucker, stop! That hurts!"

"Fine." He pushed me forward, away from him. "Pussy disgusts me anyway."

I got out of the tub and took a towel, drying myself then getting dressed again. Fresh tears ran down my face.

"Oh, it wasn't that bad, get me a towel," Carlos said.

I tossed him a towel and went into the living room. I sat on his couch holding my compact mirror, trying to reapply my heavy eye makeup. He emerged from the bathroom, wearing only the towel around his waist and a pair of flip-flops.

"You ever wear these?" he asked, holding a foot out towards me. "We always wore them in the showers at jail, because the floor was so nasty. They're so cool, you never slip or nothing."

I collected the money he owed Armando and left, praying no one would ever find out that sleaze had touched me. I went straight home. Once there I pressed play on my answering machine.

"Sweetie, it's Daddy, call me back." Zack sounded worried.

I quickly called him back, "Is everyone okay?"

"Yeah, but I gotta talk to you as soon as possible."

"Why"

"I'll tell you in person."

We made a plan to meet at a local bar after he finished work the next day. I got there hours before him, and already had a buzz on when he came to meet me. I tried to introduce him to some people there, but he was anxious to sit alone at a table with me.

"Zack, what is it?"

"Don't call me that, I'm your father, damn it!"

"Whatever ... now what's wrong?"

"I had one of those dreams of mine. It was so real." His eyes were large and when he talked like this, he seemed to have a touch of madness.

"Listen, sweetheart, you might need to get away. I mean just run, run away from here."

"No way! Where would I go?"

"Come to my house, even just for a night. Go anywhere. Just get away. Get away!"

"Get away from what, Dad?"

"I don't know. Something terrible ... something evil. I'm afraid for you, I'm terrified. This dream ... it was horrible."

"It was just a nightmare."

"No it wasn't." His eyes darted about to see if anyone was near us. He leaned in close to me. "Sweetheart, evil had you in its clutches. You were tortured. You begged me for help, only my hands were tied."

I laughed at my father. He was so histrionic. I didn't believe in his psychic visions.

"Laugh now, but swear to me," he reached across the table and grabbed my arm, squeezing hard, "Swear to me, swear you'll run away. If you sense danger, if things get scary, swear you'll run."

"Okay, okay, Daddy. I'll run. I promise."

A few days later Armando called me and said, "I am home, you must see me now."

I relented, and agreed he could come over to my apartment.

"I will come now, sí?"

"No, come in an hour."

I was dressed up to go to The Disco Lounge with Nikki. I called her to cancel, and told her if she wanted to go without me to tell Conner I said to make her my VIP.

"Girlfriend, call me later if you want, I might be here. Don't worry about what anyone thinks. Just follow your heart. I know he loves you."

"Thanks, girl," I said.

I used the hour to sit in the dark and smoke a joint, while I listened to Linda Ronstadt croon an old torch song. It was about her deep foolishness in love, and her inability to leave her lover despite her desire to. She suffered his blatant infidelities, and viewed herself a prisoner of sorts. She had been bewitched by a devilish rouge.

Then Armando was at my door, pulling me into his arms, hugging and kissing me. Pulling away, I insisted we sit on the couch and talk but it never happened. Before I could get any of the answers I wanted, he was carrying me to me bed, where he placed me down and leaning over me began undressing me. He mostly spoke in Spanish, saying soft words of love.

"Negrita, I promise I will never leave you alone when we are out again. I was so drunk. I am estúpido. You understand this, I am a man."

Soon we were naked under the warm covers. He was kissing my shoulders when he looked up, inches from my face, and studied my eyes.

"Chica, has anyone touched you these weeks we were apart?"

"I ... well ... we were broken up."

"What does this mean? You tell me now! Has another man touched you?"

"I didn't want to, it was a mistake." But that folly was nothing compared to the grave error I was now making. My mind raced and it showed on my face. I knew if Carlos told Armando he fucked me, and I denied it, Armando would believe me. Time seemed suspended as Armando waited for my answer. He had pulled back but was staring intently at my face. I debated saying, "Of course I wasn't with anyone!" but I hesitated too long.

He pushed me back roughly, and then grabbed my hair, pulling my head back.

"Ow, fucker, stop! Cabrón, let go of me!"

"You will tell me now, perra, now, who were you with?"

"No one!"

"You're a liar! Don't make me go find out, do not be estúpida, puta!"

"It was just once, for one minute ... it was bad, it was horrible. I want to forget it all. We were broken up, please, don't do this." I started crying.

Armando stood up and looked at me with disgust. He started to dress.

"No, please don't go." I was sobbing now.

He took my face with one hand and squeezed it hard. "Mira, perra, you will tell me who now, or I will break all your bones. Every one."

"It ... it was Carlos ... but he made me, I didn't want to."

"*Eres una puta repugnante*! You make me sick. I will not touch you again, not ever! You are now *sucia* ... you are *basura* ... trash. You will be so sorry you would cross me like this."

"Please, Armando, please don't go, we can talk. I didn't cross you, I swear."

He stood in the doorway to my darkened bedroom with his coat over his arm and his shoes in his hand. The contrasting hallway light obscured his face.

"I will not ever come to your bed again."

I heard him walk down the hall, pause to put his shoes on, and then open and close the front door. There was a loud click when he turned the bolt from outside the door with his key. Later, when I walked down the hall to get the phone and call Nikki, I saw a brass key on the floor. Armando had pushed it under the door after he locked it.

Nikki and I sat on my bed drinking straight from a bottle of Vodka and eating Fritos. We snorted lines of coke together, since I was desperate to stop my seemingly uncontrollable tears.

"Why did you tell him?"

"Nikki, I don't know. I guess I just wanted to hurt him. I was so humiliated when he left me at The Lounge that night. That's our place, everyone knows us. I didn't know he would take it like that, we were broken up."

"Oy, muñeca, he's a Latino man. You're lucky he didn't cut your face."

For two days Armando did not return my beeps. I called his pager twenty times a day. I stayed home each night, pacing, worrying about where he was, what he was saying, and what would become of me? Nikki stayed in with me, bringing over Mexican food and liquor. I kept her high on blow but after the night Armando left me, I didn't touch it. I was afraid he'd find out. Plus, it made my hangovers ten times worse.

On the third day, Armando called me.

I worked hard to look okay, using makeup to disguise eyes swollen from days of crying. I appeared at his house smiling, hoping he might forgive me, forgetting about all the ways he'd wronged me. I was ready to do any penance requested by him.

"Sit." He pointed to a chair and I sat as told. His manor was cold and formal. It was obvious his anger had not cooled a jot.

"Mira, we need to work together, that's why I called you. But I cannot have some puta messing around with my people. It is bad for business. You must learn to respect me."

"I respect you. I swear to god, I'll swear on anything I'll never do anything like that again. Please, Armando, don't you love me anymore? I still love you."

"No, I no longer love you. You are nothing to me."

"Why are you punishing me so much?" My composure was lost. Fresh tears rolled down my face. "But what about protection, you know I can't work without it?"

"You can always ask your new boyfriend."

"I have no new boyfriend, Armando. Please, please don't do this to me—to us."

"Here is a quarter ki," he tossed me a cellophane wrapped chunk, "call me when it is done."

As I stuffed the coke into my bag, he went and opened the front door. He made no eye contact as I slunk past him.

A few days later I delivered a few ounces to Carlos while Mateo sat in my car nearby. I tossed the ounces on the coffee table and perched on a windowsill while I waited for payment for the last delivery.

"So chica, I hear Armando is through with you."

"I guess. Carlos, do you have my money? I gotta go."

"What did you tell him, about us?"

"Nothing."

He walked over to me and stood close with a serene smile. "Chica, la linda." He reached out and stoked my hair. Then, he slapped my face.

"Ow! Cabrón, motherfucker, what are you doing?"

"I can't stand a lying puta. Armando told me you told him about us. Now, he's not gonna protect you from me. No one is."

"Carlos, you hurt me, now you're trying to scare me. What do you want?"

"I want that you will now be my bitch, my business partner."

"No, no way."

"Sí. I already told Armando and he agreed with my idea. You and I will each chip in, and he will sell us half a kilo for twenty-thousand, that's seven grand off."

"I only have five-thousand saved," I said.

"Okay, I'll put in fifteen grand."

"You have fifteen grand?"

"Sí, I been kickin' it all over this town for months."

"Then why do you get fronts?"

"I'd rather risk my brother-in-law's money, he can spare it."

"I'm not going to be your partner, and I won't be hit by you either, maricón!"

"Okay, I'm sorry, right, we'll just break the half ki up, and I'll take mine and you take yours."

"Why is Armando helping us?"

"He's not, he gets cash upfront. It's better for him. Plus, he said he doesn't care what the hell you do anymore. Or what happens to you."

Twenty-Three

Bullet: A small, hollow cylinder made of plastic or metal and shaped like a bullet. It unscrews in the middle and has a small hole in the top. You put cocaine inside and hold it slightly inside of one nostril. A hard sniff delivers a hit of coke.

I drove over to Armando's house when summoned again a few days later. His eyes were unlit pools of black, the warmth of recognition gone. He was eerily civil.

"I am going to give you the half ki in a few days, when Nikki—when my next shipment comes in. Will you collect the cash from Carlos?" he said.

"Sí, I will, but why do you want to do this?"

"To help you make more money. You always say I do not pay you enough."

"I don't care about that now!" I sat down on his sofa and started to cry.

"Chica, every time with the tears. We need to work." He sighed and looked at me with annoyance.

"I know, Armando, but how can I just mean nothing to you now? You and me were broken up, and it wasn't my fault. Carlos forced me … he hurt me … please, can't we try again?"

"Never. *Jamás te amaré*. I cannot love a whore. Lourdes was a virgin when I married her."

"But I wasn't, and you said you loved me."

"How can I love you when I feel only … *repulsión*?"

I left and drove to Nikki's. We went to an Italian restaurant called Sabatino's. It was becoming my new haunt when Armando was in town. I was scared I'd see him at La Casa with a girl and break down in public, so I only went there when he was in Florida.

Sabatino's was small and dimly lit. It was easy to pick a corner booth and disappear behind tall panels of dark wood. I ordered a bottle of white wine and ravioli, but I could barely get one bite down.

"Girlfriend, my poor girl … did you see him today?"

"I did, and he was horrible. He totally humiliated me. How much begging and crying can I do?" I didn't mention that he had called me repulsive. "I think he hates me now, Nik."

"Nah, chica, his pride is just hurt. You're too valuable to him; you made him a rich man. He's not gonna get rid of you."

"Do you mean … I mean … do you think I'll get him back?"

She looked down at her plate. "I doubt you'll ever be his girlfriend again."

I pulled out my new bullet and took a hard sniff of coke then passed it to her.

"Wait, you got a bullet? You hardly even party."

"I need it so I can hit it before I see Armando, you know, so I won't cry. He gets mad when I cry."

I signaled the waiter and ordered a second bottle of wine.

"Nikki, I have made a big mistake … fucking huge."

The next morning I awoke to banging on my door. It was Carlos.

"Putaña, time to get up." He pushed past me holding a white paper bag and went to my kitchen. "Mira, I brought you hot chocolate and a pastry. There's a really good place on your corner."

"What the fuck? How did you get into my hallway? Chulo, you can't just show up without calling."

"I'm the man, *el rey*! I can do whatever I want, puta."

"You have to leave."

"That's the thanks I get for bringing you breakfast? And for feeding your undercovers?"

"My what?"

"You know, the detectives sitting in front of your house."

I ran down the hall to my bedroom, and looked out onto the street through the window. There were two men sitting in a parked car. Carlos came up behind me and looked over my shoulder.

"See, there they are. I brought them coffee and doughnuts. Everyone knows cops love that, and it's polite to take care of them."

A few hours later, I left my house, forgetting about the detectives. But when I pulled away from the curb I noticed a car also pull out. Looking in my review mirror, I recognized the two men Carlos had pointed out. They followed me diligently, until it was an unmistakable fact I was being tailed.

Speeding and getting far ahead of them, I drove to a rural road and went fast along its many curves. I pulled off near a patch of bushes, backing my car in and facing the road. I turned off the engine and slid down on the seat, watching the road through my steering wheel. Minutes later, I saw the men pass my hiding spot in hot pursuit. I laughed at them, and then drove off in the opposite direction.

By the days end, I'd forgotten about them completely.

Less than a week later, I had Mateo drive me to Armando's. I had a pile of cash in my purse I'd picked up from Carlos the night before. I used the bullet on the drive over, snorting coke hits until I felt sure I wouldn't cry.

I was only at Armando's a few minutes. He sat in silence counting the piles of money I'd placed on the table. I chain smoked Marlboro lights.

"Okay, sí, bueno," he said when he finished.

"Armando, should I use this coke for your customers, or are you going to give me more?"

"No, just use that."

"But there will be more profit."

"I'll just give you a bigger cut."

"This is not making sense. Why should you lose money?"

"I take care of myself, it will make sense if you think some. Now, you must go, I'm leaving for Florida today."

I stumbled out the door with dry eyes. Mateo drove me to my safe house, where I placed the half ki inside the safe. Walking out through Janet's kitchen, I tossed a chunk of cocaine and a fifty-dollar bill on the table. She thanked me and scooped up both with her free hand. In her other arm was a little girl with a bottle.

I got back in the car with Mateo. "Mat, do you want to make some extra money tonight?"

"Sí, sí."

"I need to come back here tonight and package. I have so many orders it's gonna take hours, so I thought you could help me. Then, we need to drop Carlos his share and spend all night on deliveries."

I was about to make a ton of cash, maybe even the most I'd ever made in one night. Money comforted me, when I had it I felt invulnerable. Wads of cash in my purse made me giddy. Money killed pain faster than any drug I knew.

Mateo brought me home and I gave him my car to use. "Pick me up at seven for dinner at La Casa. You can come have dinner with us, I'm meeting Carlos," I said.

"Carlos, por qué? You're a crazy girl."

"I know, I know."

I was meeting Carlos to discuss the plan for the coke delivery, but dinner was unnecessary. I agreed to it because underneath the outward show of camaraderie, I was plotting to somehow diffuse him.

At La Casa that night, walking down a narrow hall towards the dining room, I watched myself in the large gold-framed mirrors that hung along the walls. I wore black leather: tight leather pants, a soft leather tee, tall leather boots with wicked heels, and a full-length leather coat. I also wore jewelry. Large gold rings on all four fingers of each hand, and multiple gold chains of different lengths with 24-karat gold charms dangling from them; my florid initial, a tiny star, a heart trimmed with diamonds Armando had given me, and a tinselly cross.

As I admired myself, I had no idea I would never again see the girl I was that night. I smiled at my reflection. I was successful and deludedly self-assured. I felt powerful, and I emulated my idols perfectly; I was a world-class liar, I was secretive, I was stoic about my business affairs, I had a massive ego, and I had a mean, vengeful streak.

When I approached the table that seated my posse, there sat Armando and Peter, his limo driver.

"Chica, cómo estás?" he said, hardly looking at me.

"Bien." I sat down nervously.

During dinner, Armando sat next to Carlos, talking only in Spanish. I ignored them and watched my pager screen repeatedly display phone numbers. All of my customers were Jonesing.

I got up and walked over to a row of pay phones lining the wall near the restrooms. I sat on a red velvet stool and traced my fingers along the raised gold brocade wallpaper while I made calls. "Janet, it's me. I should be there within the hour and listen; I'm bringing Mateo, my driver. He's totally cool."

"Okay, I guess." she said.

Next I called my friend Anita. "Anita, you paged me like fifty times!"

"Girl, I'm sorry. I just gotta get something, you know. Raúl has been giving me nothing but shit." Raúl was her pimp.

"Can't you get it from Jamal? I don't do small, you know that."

"I know, but just this once, as a favor to your girl. You can give it to me cheaper than him. Come on, chica, I'll buy an eight-ball."

"Okay, okay. I'll come soon."

I added her to my order book. I spun around on the stool to find Armando standing behind me.

"I want you to come with me," he said.

"Where?" For a moment I was excited. I wanted us to make up so badly. But then my gut surged with fear. He had not spoken a friendly word or even looked at me directly for weeks. Why the urgent need to talk now?

"I'm going to the Airport in my limo. Take the ride with me and we will talk."

"I don't think I can, I have so much work tonight."

"Please, chica, just come."

"Lemme think about it while I go to the ladies room."

I sat at the vanity in the bathroom and took a hit from my bullet, trying to squelch the emerging tears. This was a moment I'd longed for—Armando wanted to talk to me! But what if this was a ruse and I ended up in an unmarked grave, or floating in the ocean? What if Zack's nightmares were about this very moment? I never had any evidence Armando was dangerous, less the stash of guns, the threats of beatings, and his claims that he aspired to be Scarface. But my belly screamed, "No!"

As I approached the table he got up and came towards me so we were speaking privately.

"Well, will you come as I ask?"

"I want to, I really do, but I just can't tonight. You know why, you restocked me today. My pager is going nuts. I promised people. Can we talk when you come back? I really want to, I swear."

"Sí, okay." He looked sad for a moment, then he called out to Peter and they left.

I left La Casa shortly after Armando left for the airport. Carlos followed me out to the parking lot.

"Hey," I called to him from the open window of my car, "can you loan me an eight-ball?" I figured it would be quicker to drop it to Anita on the way to my safe house.

Without a word he tossed it through the open window and onto my lap.

I stuck the eight ball in my bra, and Mateo took me to Anita's house.

"Chica, I love you, you came," she kissed and hugged me, swaying slightly on her feet.

"Nita, I gotta run. Gimme two-fifty."

"You're fucking kidding! Girl, I love you so much, you are so good to me." She hugged me again, tightly. She was an Amazon, nearly six feet tall, with huge gold bamboo earrings and long, decorated nails.

She handed me the cash and I shoved it in my pocket. It was far too typical and much too small to have been the last coke deal I would ever make.

Mateo and I drove on to my safe house, arriving around 10 p.m. Probably around the same time as the town police and the DEA began to converge in the parking lot of a nearby strip mall that was closed for the night. Later, a friend told me he drove by and thought there was a break-in at the mall, there were so many cop cars parked there.

PART THREE

Twenty-Four

Walking into Janet's, we were careful to keep quiet. Her little boy and girl were asleep in the second bedroom. She led us into her bedroom, where she locked her door and sat on the bed.

I opened the thick door to my silver safe. Twelve thousand dollars sat neatly bound with an elastic band. This was money I did not invest. It was my savings. I removed the plastic-wrapped block of cocaine I had placed there earlier that day, two razor blades, a box of sandwich bags, a roll of tin foil and two electronic scales. Mateo set up two small workstations on top of the dresser.

I removed the plastic wrap from the brick. I asked Janet to grab me a plate. She did, and I dropped the naked block of white onto it. I took a razor blade and began slicing powdery chunks off. I tossed a tiny chunk of cocaine to Janet. She promptly grabbed a mirror and began cutting up lines, then snorting them through a rolled twenty-dollar bill.

I retrieved the coded notebook from my purse that listed my current orders. "Here," I said as I handed a chunk of coke to Mateo, "make three ounces." Each ounce was pushed into the corner of the sandwich bag, tied into a knot and the excess plastic pulled until it ripped off, creating a small perfect ball of white.

"Girl, how late are you gonna work here? I gotta sleep because the kids wake me up early," Janet said.

"Sleep in the living room," I said. "I'll probably be here another hour." I ripped off small pieces of foil and folded it around single grams for my friends.

"I'll wait," Janet said and left the bedroom, returning with a can of beer.

An hour later, I started getting ready to leave. I pulled my shirt up, and placed an eight-ball in my bra. All of the packaged coke would be hidden on my body: in my bra, boots, underwear, and pockets.

I heard a distant tinkling sound, like glass breaking. I pulled my shirt down and looked at Janet.

"It's the cops!" Janet said.

The three of us froze and stood in silence for what felt like hours. Silently, I prayed we were being robbed. Then we heard a loud crash and the unmistakable sounds of smashing glass.

Mateo stepped towards the bedroom window. "Let's get the fuck out of here," he said.

Tiny bits of glass suddenly sprayed all over him. My mind reeled trying to create an explanation for what I was seeing. Within seconds a man lunged through the window with a shotgun in his hand. I turned towards the bedroom door but before I could take even one step, the entire door came crashing down. I could hear the kids screaming in the background, as men with black baseball caps and dark blue jackets rushed through the door.

The men were yelling, "Get on the floor! Get on the fucking floor, now!" They never identified themselves, so I continued to hope we were getting jacked. We all lay on the floor as they continued to yell, "Face down, put your face to the floor!" I could no longer see anything. A heavy boot stepped on my back and the metal of a gun was pressed to my skull. My arms were grabbed and pulled behind my back. I was being handcuffed. My mind was still racing, but I couldn't feel a thing.

"You're under arrest. You have the right to remain silent," said one of the men, as he began reading us our rights.

We were busted.

I was pulled to my feet. The men now seemed more relaxed. They talked to each other as if we were invisible. A man walked past me pulling Mateo along and I saw large, white stamped letters on the back of his windbreaker that said DEA.

"You take her, Sam," a DEA man directed the town police officer who had walked into the bedroom in regular uniform. The DEA man seemed to be in charge. He walked around the room, calmly stating orders. "Jack, call Child Protective Services, Dave, take the guy in your car. Is there a neighbor we can get to come stay with the kids?" The kids were still screaming and crying in the next room. Janet told them to call their father and he'd come take them.

Sam took me, as directed. We stopped in the kitchen, and the DEA man stared at me. I smiled nervously. He looked like he could be one of us, with his beard and longish dark curls. He was young, and he looked like Cat Stevens, whose face graced an album cover I often kissed when I was twelve.

I looked around the room and saw that every window had been smashed, and the door to the kitchen broken in. I could see into the kid's room. There was a carpet of glass on the floor below the window. Men with shotguns walked around the house, glass crunching under their black boots. A cluster of them stood talking in Janet's bedroom. I heard her crying, begging them to let her go to the kids. Instead, she was led into the kitchen where she shot me a look of hate. We each had a town cop holding us by the arm. The DEA man told them to take us away, and we were led to separate cop cars.

The cop I was with drove off. As we traveled, he asked me if I was okay.

"Yeah, I guess."

"How did you get mixed up in this crowd?" he asked.

"I was just there, I don't know. Why are you arresting us, I mean, where are the Southbridge cops?"

"You're one mile over the city line, we're going to the Leicester town police station."

At the station, I was uncuffed by a tall, handsome young officer. He took my hand. "I'm going to fingerprint you now, so relax your hand." As he rolled my fingers one at a time, first through ink, then over paper, I leaned into him. He said in a low voice, "Got yourself into some trouble, huh?"

"I'm having fun now."

"Fun?"

"Yes, this feels good." I stared at his face, waiting for a reaction.

He smiled, but didn't look at me. After he finished fingerprinting me, he walked me to an empty cell. "You need to go in here."

"Are you coming with me?"

"No ... I ... I have to go to my desk." He seemed nervous and a little shy.

"Well, I'll miss you."

"Turn around please," he said.

I did and he started to place handcuffs on me.

"No, please ... my wrists hurt," I said.

"I'm sorry, miss, I'll get in trouble."

"Okay then." I stepped backwards until I was pressed into him. He pushed me forward and clicked the cuffs on.

200

"I'll ask Sarge if I can take them off of you."

"Thanks, sweetie."

"My name is officer Smith."

He closed the bar-clad door and locked me in. A short, stout woman in a police uniform came rushing up. "I have to search the prisoner before you put her in there!"

My heart pounded, as I contemplated the eight-ball stashed in my bra.

An officer leaned out of a door to an office across from my cell. "Leave her. You don't need to search her, she's just a kid."

"Okay, Sergeant."

They walked away and the Sergeant disappeared.

I sat down on the bench that was also a bed. I had to get rid of the coke, because I knew eventually they would strip-search me. I reached up my back underneath my shirt with my wrists still handcuffed. Swallowing the pain, I groped for my bra strap. Catching it, I tugged it down and released the hook with my fingers. The plastic wrapped ball of cocaine rolled down my belly and landed in my lap. I stood up, and it fell on the floor. I kicked it under the bunk, into the shadows of the cell.

Just as I sat back down, the tall cop, who told me his name was officer Smith, returned. "Sarge wants to see you," he said.

I walked out of the cell and across the hall. As I walked into the Sergeant's office, I smiled at him. He smiled back.

"Uncuff her," he said to Smith.

Smith removed the handcuffs and left, closing the door. I stood rubbing my wrists.

"Have a seat, little girl," he said. He smiled lasciviously.

I sat down across the desk, debating just how far I would go to get out of going to jail.

"What's a pretty little thing like you doing all mixed up with these characters?"

"I'm not mixed up, Carl."

"Carl! How do you know that?" He chuckled.

I gestured at the nameplate on his desk. "Or should I call you Sergeant Conroy?"

He shook his head. "Carl is fine."

I leaned over his desk towards him. "Do you have a wife, Carl?"

"Yes."

"Too bad." I picked up a scrap of paper from his desk and kissed it, making a print with my lipstick. "Here. So you'll remember me."

"Oh, I'll remember you." He placed the paper in his desk drawer.

Then I heard a familiar voice, loudly cursing in Spanish and protesting in English. It was Carlos. "Vete pa' carajo, I got my rights! You can't just arrest me, I want my lawyer!" He howled and bellowed.

"Carl, can I open the door to your office?" I asked in my most sugary voice.

"There's nothing out there for you."

"I just want to see, please?"

He walked over and held the heavy wooden door open with one arm. I stood behind him, peering over his arm. When I placed my chin on it, he quickly dropped his hand and walked away, sitting back down at his desk.

I leaned out the door.

"Stay in here, please. You're a minor."

"Carl, look, both my feet are inside your office." Looking down the long hall, I could see Carlos being fingerprinted. Then Smith led him down the hall to where I stood.

"Miss, step back inside Sergeant Conroy's office."

I did, but I left the door open a crack and peeked out. Sergeant Conroy was talking on the telephone at his desk. I watched Smith lock

Carlos in the same jail cell I'd been in, the only one in the station. Smith walked away and Carlos put his face to the bars and clenched his teeth.

"Talk, and you die, puta."

"I would never talk to pigs, you know that," I said.

I heard Janet and Mateo being brought into the station. I closed the door and sat back down across from the sergeant, who was now filling out pages of documents. I heard the creaking of the cell door. I jumped up and peeked out the door and saw Janet and Mateo being placed in the cell with Carlos.

"Sergeant? Why aren't I in there with them?"

"You're a minor and I only have one cell. Bad enough I have males in there with a female, but since you're all friends—"

"What's gonna happen?"

"You're all going to see the judge."

"But it's 2:00 a.m.!"

"Judges never sleep."

"Why is Carlos here?"

"Stop with the questions, you're in a lot of trouble you know."

"Can I draw?"

He gave me paper and a few pens and I sat doodling.

The sergeant left the room. I heard his shoes tap the marble floor as he walked down the hall. I stood in the doorway again and called to my friends.

"Hey, psst!"

They all came near the bars.

"There's an eight-ball in the cell, under the bench. You guys gotta get rid of it," I said.

Carlos rushed to the back of the cell emerged with it in his hand. He ripped the plastic open. There was enough coke there to get eight people high, but the three of them literally stuffed it up their noses and even ate some of it. They flushed the plastic down the toilet. We all started laughing and joking. Smith showed up.

"What are you doing?" he asked me.

Before I could answer, Carlos started talking. "You should fuck her man, she's sexy, look at her pants. Don't you just want to grab her?"

Smith ignored Carlos and turned to me. "Sarge wants you to stay in his office with the door closed."

"I'm lonely, you come in here with me." As I reached for him he drew back. My friends laughed loudly, wasted on cocaine. Smith pushed me back into the office and closed the door.

I went over and opened the Sergeant's desk drawer. Before I could rifle, he came in. Amused, he asked what I was looking for.

"Nothing. Carl, I'm bored."

"Sit back down in that chair," he said.

I plopped back into the chair and he sat down across from me again trying to look stern but really, looking curious. "What are you doing with that riffraff? None of those men respect you."

"Oh, and you do?"

"Not really, but I would still treat you a thousand times better."

"Is that an offer?"

He smiled and started to write again. His phone rang. "Hello? Yes, she's right here. I'll bring her myself."

"Bring me where?"

He took me by the arm. "Come on, princess."

We walked down the hall, and he placed me alone in a tiny, dimly lit room with a small table and two chairs. I sat down at the table. Minutes later, I heard someone come in. I didn't turn around. He walked over, put a briefcase on the table and sat down. It was Cat Stevens, the DEA agent.

"Hello, my name is Michael." He spoke softly. "These are my files … files on you." He started to remove folders, fat folders full of papers and black and white photos. He put the briefcase on the floor and spread some of the photos out on the table.

"Here you are with Armando, with Carlos, in Miami, in front of your house, getting into a limo." He shuffled through the photos. "Are you going to go to prison for these scumbags?"

I was silent. He started getting angry, and his voice got louder. "You aren't like these people. We all know it, why don't you?"

I wondered why everyone kept saying that to me.

"Do you have any gum?" I asked. He ignored my question. "You know, you look like Cat Stevens, who I was in love with."

"Are you going to talk to me, or are you going to prison for lowlifes who will end up killing you?"

"Listen, I don't know what you're talking about, but there's this old movie I saw, from the forties, where a cop observes a woman while working as a detective, and he falls in love with her … are you married?"

He shoved all the papers and photos on the floor with a sweep of his arm, and then stood up quickly, knocking over his chair. "You do not understand the severity of this situation, young lady! You are going to prison—maybe for life!"

"What's it to you? Unless you love me."

"Listen up, little girl, you can be home in your bed tonight. No jail, not even for a night."

"When do I see my lawyer? In the movies, you get a phone call. No one has let me make a call."

"You don't need a call if you talk to me."

"Okay, what do you want to talk about?"

"Armando."

"Don't know him."

"Oh no? Why don't you look these photos over while I read you one of my reports?"

I glanced disinterested at the numerous photos of Armando and me; walking down the street in Southbridge, renting a car in Miami, having dinner with a Colombian family on a terrace in an expensive restaurant.

Michael's report called me Armando's paramour. I had no idea what that meant. I interrupted him while he was describing every movement I had made on a particular day. "Isn't your job silly? Don't you care about real crime, like murders? My classmate was murdered right near here, and no one was even arrested."

An hour later, his energy was waning. It was nearly 4 a.m., and I still had not answered a single question.

"Are you ready for prison?" he said.

I thrust my hands out towards him. "Cuff me."

Michael left the room, vowing he'd see me again. "I'll visit you in jail, when you've had a few days to think."

"Okay, love you!" I called out.

A few minutes later Smith walked in. As he handcuffed me I whispered, "I'll miss you. Will you come see me?"

"Sarge might." He guided me down the hall to the Sergeants office. "I heard you want to make a call. Here's a phone."

I sat down at Carl's desk and picked up the phone. I had to think fast. Who could I call who wasn't in the business? I can't call my dealers from the police station. So I called my mother. She had Armando's number, because she cleaned his house for him. I told her I was in jail and to have my "friend" get me a lawyer.

She was cold and unsympathetic. "Yeah, well, I guess you fucked up now. I told you not to mess up with him."

"Just make the fucking call, you bitch!"

"Fine!" She slammed the phone down.

Carl told me to get ready to go see the judge and soon I was sitting handcuffed in a little waiting room in the judge's office. I sat shoulder to shoulder with my codefendants. Four cops watched over us, none of us spoke a word. We were called in separately. While Janet was inside with the judge, I turned to Carlos.

"You were not at the house with us, why are you here?"

He laughed loudly. "Stupid pendejos pulled my car over and searched it without a warrant. Then, they planted a gun on me! I'll be out by the afternoon."

A cop I didn't know called my name, and escorted me into the judge's chamber. I sat in a chair across the desk from a balding man who was busy reading papers. He looked up at me.

"I am sending you to be held in the county jail pending trial. You are charged with four felonies." He went on to read out the charges, penal codes, etc.

"Do you understand the charges against you?"

"Yes, but I'm not guilty, I didn't—"

"Quiet! Just answer the judge," the cop said.

"Yes sir."

"Good. I am sending you to jail without bail." He looked up at the cop. "You can take her now."

"Wait a minute, please, your honor, why don't I get bail?"

"I told you to keep your mouth shut!" The cop grabbed my arm and pulled me to my feet. He walked me to his car and put me in the back.

All my hopes of being bailed out later that day dissolved. No bail! This was the second time I was sent to jail with no bail. But last time, it only meant a weekend in jail. This time it meant I could be held until my trial and that could take a year. My cavalier attitude started to wear off. I suddenly felt small, and afraid.

"Where are you taking me?"

"Southbridge city jail. They'll transport you to county jail later today."

"But officer, I'm innocent, I swear."

"Shut up already, you're going to jail for a long, long time."

Twenty-Five

I was too stunned to cry and too tired to think. The sun was coming up as we arrived at the Southbridge police station. The town cop handed me over with a pile of papers to a female officer. She took my arm and led me to a small room where she told me to sit down. She left, locking me in with a loud jangle of keys. Minutes later she brought Janet in. We were patted down and then led through a thick metal door to a room containing a row of tiny cells. We were each placed in one.

"Excuse me, officer," I called out, "I'm having my period, and I need a tampon."

"Yeah, right," she called back, as she was leaving the tier.

"Oh, and officer, it is freezing in here, can we get a blanket?"

The bed was a bare metal shelf bolted onto the wall.

She snickered and said, "Of course, I'll be right back, your highness."

Janet and I lay on cold metal talking through the walls. My underwear grew wet with blood. I had never been so uncomfortable in my life.

"I've been to county before," I said to Janet, "it's not too bad."

Janet was crying. "My kids, what about my kids?"

"You'll get them back."

"How the fuck do you know? This is so bad. I'm gonna lose them, I know it."

"I'm so sorry, Janet."

"Yeah, I'm sure you are."

Five hours later the officer returned with neither blanket nor tampon. I told her my underwear were wet.

"So take them off and throw them away," she said.

"Can I have a tampon?"

"No, I don't have one. You're starting to piss me off, so just shut up. You'll get what you need at county."

"But that's a forty-five minute drive."

She opened the door to my cell and pulled me out. "I told you to shut your mouth."

Next, she released Janet from her cell.

"Now, ladies, stand still with your hands in front of you."

She placed a chain belt around my waist, which also had long chains attached to both ankle and handcuffs. Both my wrists and ankles were now braceleted with metal cuffs. She put the same on Janet.

"Now try to walk without falling," she said. We could only manage tiny, half steps.

We shuffled as directed, and she brought us outside to a large bus. We could hardly walk up the steps inside the vehicle. A male officer took over.

"Ladies, go to the back of the bus, to the last seats."

The bus was full of men, including Mateo and Carlos.

"Guys, look front, don't even look at the girls," the officer said, "and I don't want to hear a single word from anyone. All of you better keep quiet." He sat down in the seat behind the driver.

Another cop jumped on the bus holding a shotgun, and we drove off. Though nobody spoke a word, some of the guys turned to steal looks at us during the ride.

We arrived at the county jail. We were given over to female COs who fingerprinted and photographed us, stripped searched us, and took away our clothes. We were given grey prison sweat suits. Next, we were locked in the tier, a long, narrow cage with a row of sixteen tiny cells on one side. There were ten girls there that day. One girl was serving 364 days for grand theft auto, which was the judge's way of not sending her to state prison. County jail is either for people awaiting trial, or sentences lasting under a year. The car thief was named Latisha, and she soon became my best friend. She was the toughest girl there, having already done time in state prison.

The tier was a lot like a dormitory with girls braiding each other's hair, gossiping, talking about boys. Lots of them were hookers serving ten days. We all got along fine, directing our hatred at our mutual enemy: the COs.

On my second day in jail, I had a visitor. The CO took me to a small room where DEA agent Michael was sitting. She closed the door and left us alone.

"Oh, it's you."

"Were you hoping Armando would come? Missy, open your eyes, you've got no bail. He can't get you out of here, but I can."

"Okay, then get me out."

"You have to do something for me."

"Right here? Okay." I put my hand on his knee.

He took my hand off his leg and placed it back in my lap. "Look, to me you're nothing but a kid. But you're a smart kid and you're a kid who knows a lot. I can take you home now, today, if you will talk to me."

"About what?"

"Armando. That's who I want. Look at all the damage he does, don't you want to do the right thing?"

"I don't know him."

"That's bullshit and you know it! He's your boyfriend. I've spent two years watching you and him. I know he cheats on you with hookers, and for god's sake—he's married! He's twenty years older than you. You have no life with him. Look, I know your Mother abandoned you, I know about your family. But I swear, I can help you. I can help you get an apartment and get into college. You always said you wanted to be a writer."

"Wait, how do you know that?"

"I know a lot about you and I want to be your friend. Please, let me be your friend."

"Why do you care so much?" My eyes filled with tears. I looked hard at my sneakers, trying not to cry.

"Because I told you, you're special. You're not like the others."

"I don't know what you mean."

"I know you don't, but if you'll just trust me you will know, I promise."

"Michael, I don't know anything, I can't help you."

We sat together without speaking. I sniffled and he handed me a tissue from his pocket.

"Look, I'll come back tomorrow. Think of what you might want to do with your life. Do you want to spend it like this, in prison for some man who doesn't give a fuck about you or what happens to you?"

I looked up, startled. That was practically verbatim what Carlos had said to me.

I returned to staring at my shoes and he pushed a buzzer for the CO.

"I'll be back tomorrow. Think about it, okay?"

I didn't answer him.

About two hours later the CO came and called my name again. "You're popular today," she said. She led me to the same small room, only this time, there was a suit waiting for me.

"Hi, I'm David Lowenthal. I'm your lawyer, your friend hired me."

"Thank god! Can you get me out of here?"

"Well, by law they have seven days to set bail. I'll go to your bail hearing with you and get it as low as possible. Now tell me, has the DEA been here?"

"Yes, Michael was just here a few hours ago."

"Okay, that will be the end of that. I'll bar all visits. They won't be able to question you anymore without me there. Now, have you told them anything?"

"Not a word."

"Good girl. Now tell me everything they've asked you."

Michael never came back, just as David promised. A week later, I was shackled wrists and ankles and taken in chains to my bail hearing at a court on the grounds of the jail. After much debate between the prosecutor, who insisted I was a flight risk, and David, who personally promised I'd be there for my trial, the judge set my bail for one million dollars.

I turned to my lawyer, shocked. "David, I'll never get out with that kind of bail!"

The CO came to take me away.

"David!"

"Don't worry," he said, "you'll get another hearing in a week."

"A week! Another fucking week in that pit?"

"I'm sorry. You're in a lot of trouble, you've been charged with four felonies and you're facing two life sentences. I did my best kiddo, I swear. Don't worry. I'll see you next week."

Twenty-Six

Roll: When a criminal talks to the police and gives evidence or information on another criminal in order to get themselves out of trouble.

"Seely!" I stood up from the plastic table we sat at together during visits. The room was set up like a classroom, only with a guard instead of a teacher supervising the room. "You're my girl, how do you get here so much?"

"Well, I, you know ... I can get anywhere I need."

"Don't tell me you're hitchhiking."

"I have to sis, there's no other way."

"Fuck, Seel, what about Angela? Some psycho could pick you up."

"I'm careful, I swear."

"I don't want you to stop coming, I'd die, but I'm scared for you."

Seely came almost every day. She was my only visitor, but I was lucky. Few girls got any visitors at all. It was the only respite I got from the tiny cell I was locked in twelve hours a day, and the narrow caged hallway outside the cell I spent the other twelve in. Jail is not prison. There is no yard, no recreation, no job, no school, no nothing. There is a small black and white TV, a gaggle of girls to talk to, and plenty of hair crème and combs to pass the day. If you want books, someone has to bring them to you and you get them from the guards after they've been searched.

Seely's eyes filled with tears.

"Seel, what's wrong?" I asked her.

"I'm scared for you, sissy. People are saying things ... bad things. And Carlos is out. What's gonna happen to you?"

"Nothing will happen to me, don't worry. But I need you to deliver a message. Tell Armando I said for him to come and see me."

"Should you see him, I mean, are you sure you want to?"

"I just need you to do it."

"Okay, I will."

"Now, you gotta tell me all the gossip from out there." I patted her hand and she passed me a note, which was against the rules.

"It's from Nikki. She loves you, and so do I. Remember what I wrote in your yearbook, BOSF."

"Yeah, best of sisters forever."

Joan came to see me once. She sat with her arms crossed, looking mad.

"What's your problem?" I asked her.

"I can't believe you fucked up so bad, what's wrong with you?"

"Ma, I hate you, you hate me, so why don't you just fucking leave. I don't know why you even came."

She left in a huff. But she occasionally sent me care packages, with clothes I was allowed to wear and cookies I shared with the girls. She

216

even sent money with Seely, which was deposited into my commissary account. I used it to buy peanut butter and jelly crackers, shampoo, soap, and cigarettes for Latisha.

Then, Armando came.

"Hey Chica."

"Fuck you, cabrón! I've been sitting here a month and your stupid lawyer only got my bail down to $800,000."

"Hey, he cost me twenty grand. He's muy bueno, I promise."

"Mira, the *federales* told me all they want is you. I never said a single word. I told them I didn't know you, even though they have pictures of us. Pictures of us in Florida!"

"Puta mierda ... for real?"

"Sí. They've been taking pictures for years. Remember that guy you saw take your picture? He was DEA."

"Eso se coge para arriba!"

"Whatever, yeah it sucks, but right now I'm freaking because Seely says that people are saying I rolled. Why the fuck are they saying that when you know for a fact I didn't?"

"No sé."

"Well, I'm sitting here rotting in jail. If I rolled I'd be home in my bed. Someone is spreading rumors. David knows everything, he's my fucking lawyer and you're paying him."

"Sí, sí. I'll tell them."

"I'm serious Armando, I could be free right now if I roll on you, but I would never do that."

"I know, I know, gracias. Mira, I will go to David's office today and tell him he has to get your bail down."

"Then you'll bail me out? He says you only need to put down ten percent and a bondsman will get me out."

"Sí, I will."

"And come see me again, *por favor*. I gotta get out of that goddamn cell."

"I will return soon." He kissed my hands and left.

I was led back to the tier. A few hookers I particularly liked had arrived again for another short stint, so there was a party atmosphere. A group of us gathered in my cell after dinner for story time, a nightly event I'd organized where the hookers told us tales of the craziest Johns they'd been with. It was like an x-rated slumber party. Latisha sat on my bed rubbing my shoulders while I sat on the floor.

Janet poked her head in. "I heard Armando was here today."

"Yeah, he was."

"Did you tell him he's gotta get me a lawyer too?"

"I told him, girl. He's all claiming he's broke." I said, lying. I meant to tell Armando he had to help her, but I was so obsessed with getting out I only thought of myself when I saw him.

"Well, I haven't talked, I haven't said shit, and I lost my kids!"

"I know, I know, Janet. But they are with their father, he's a good guy, right?"

She stared at me fuming, her eyes full of hate.

"Listen, I'm so sorry … I'll work on it, I swear."

"That line is so tired. Why don't you tell him that I'm here, protecting his little bitch, and he needs to help me?"

"Okay, that's enough mouth," Latisha said. "I know you're upset, and you lost your babies and shit, but you don't need to be giving my girl a hard time. She's in it with you."

"You don't know nothing, Latisha, you don't even have kids. And she's just using you. That's what she does; she's a total user. Just give her some time, she'll burn you too."

Latisha jumped up off the bed, her Reeboks squealed on the marble floor. Janet ran. I grabbed Latisha's pant leg. "Tish, just leave her, she's really got it rough."

"Yeah, but that don't mean she can talk shit about my girl."

"Just come back," I said, "She's okay. She lost everything, you don't understand."

"No, you don't understand, girlfriend. She did the crime, now she's paying. That's not your fault; she's a grown woman. We all gots to pay if we play. And you're too soft, whatcha gonna do if you end up in state with her? You gonna kiss her ass for the next five years?"

"Please, babe, just let it go. It'll be alright," I said. "I just wanna hear the rest of Peaches' story about the John in ladies underwear."

Latisha sat back down and placed her arms around me, leaning over, hugging me from behind. I turned and kissed her. "I promise, Tish, I'll take care of myself."

"Babygirl, you don't know shit about prison. You owe a debt to some bitch, she'll fuck you up, and she'll have friends in there, it ain't gonna be like here. I ain't gonna be there to protect you."

Twenty-Seven

Zack came to visit a few times looking sad. He lectured me, saying, "I told you something bad was gonna happen. Why didn't you listen?"

Then, one day he came in and said, "Honey, I have great news!"

"You do, daddy?"

"Yes, you can get out of jail on bail if I put up my house. But you have to come and live with Leona and me. You'll be completely under my control. You won't even be allowed out. But you'll be out of jail."

"No way."

"Are you serious? You'd rather stay in jail than live with your own Father?"

"You mean my own Father as my jailer and his evil wife. At least here the guards don't have a personal grudge against me."

"Leona doesn't hate you, that's ridiculous."

"She totally hates me, she's always been jealous of me. I'm sorry, Daddy, but I won't be safe at your house and I'm not gonna be your prisoner—no fucking way! Just get me out of here and I promise I won't jump bail."

"No, no, I can't. I can't risk my house."

"I said I promise I won't jump bail. Besides, Leona will probably plant drugs on me and call the cops, and then I'll go away forever."

"I can't risk my house and then let you just go back to Southbridge, to hang out with those bastards who got you in this trouble."

"Then just leave because you're not my father!"

He stood up, looking stricken. And right then, with the worst timing ever, Armando strolled into visiting and came over to my table. My father stared him down like a mad dog. Armando looked frightened, which I thought strange.

"Stay away from my daughter. Do you hear me? Stay away from her—and from Seely!"

Armando stood speechless. He'd never even seen my father before.

"Officer Mulvey," I called to the CO that supervised the visiting room, "Will you remove this man? He's causing problems." I pointed to my father.

"Come on sir, you have to leave." My father looked at me with shock as he was escorted out of the room.

"Oh, and officer Mulvey? I want him banned from visits."

I had the right to ban any visitor I didn't want to see.

Armando sat down. "That's your *padre*?"

"Sí."

"He's scary."

"You're crazy, he's just an old hippie."

"Yes, but his eyes *me penetra*. He hates me, how does he know me?"

"He doesn't know you. He doesn't know shit."

"I think he loves you very much."

"Yeah, right. So, are you here to bail me out?"

"No, sorry, chica, I cannot."

"But my bail is only $400,000. Surely you have forty grand to put up for me?"

"No, I don't. The lawyer cost me twenty."

"Mira, you bail me out, or else."

"Just give me a little more time."

"I've been in this rat hole almost three months!"

"Soon, I promise, soon."

Time dragged on. The head of the jail, Sheriff Lange, made weekly tours through the ladies section of the jail. The guards would yell, "Male on tier!" That meant we were supposed to be dressed. Some of the hookers remained in their underwear, just to fuck with him. He was a tall, bulky man in his thirties, with thick graying hair and a large gut hanging over his belt. He would walk slowly down the hall, looking through the bars at us and saying things like, "Damn, lots of fine pussy wasted in here. It's a real shame." He seemed to get off on humiliating us.

There were night raids. A siren would go off, and all the lights would come on. They usually took place around 3 a.m. The water would be shut off, so we couldn't flush anything down our toilets. We never had any contraband to flush anyway. We were all escorted to the end of the tier and herded into the shower area. While we were stripped and cavity searched by the females COs, a band of male COs would rip our cells apart. They'd throw our books, clothes, mattresses and toiletries around, and rip down our wall hangings, mostly pictures from magazines ripped out and tacked up with chewing gum.

They never found anything. After they finished we'd be sent back to our cells and locked in again, where we'd spend the next hour cleaning up and putting our beds back together so we could sleep.

Seely came in one day looking nervous and I knew as soon as I saw her she had bad news.

"Seely, just tell me," I said, as she sat on the plastic bench across from me.

"It's a nice spring day, sissy. I wish you could see outside. The sky is so blue."

"I don't give a fuck about the sky, Seel. I know you have bad news, so just tell me now."

"Well ... I can't. You're gonna freak out and it's bad enough in here as it is."

"Yeah, but now that I know something is wrong you gotta tell me, or I will fucking freak."

"Okay, okay ... it's Jamal. I'm so sorry ... he ... he died."

"What are you talking about?"

"He had some weird virus, the doctors don't really know, and some of his brothers might have it too, they think, they're not sure. They put a quarantine sign on his house."

"What the fuck are you talking about?" I started to cry. "Seely, he must've OD'ed, people don't die from viruses, that's, like, the flu or something."

"I don't know. I just know he's dead and I'm really sorry."

Twenty-Eight

Cooled: To be kept in jail for a period of time. Used by officials to break a person down into giving evidence about or confessing to a crime.

Drop Dime: To rat someone out to the police or authorities. The term comes from the act of putting a dime in a payphone to make a call.

Almost three months to the day I was arrested, my bail was dropped to one hundred thousand dollars. I shuffled back to my cell and began to pack.

"You really gonna leave me here?" Janet stood at the door to my cell.

"I'm sorry, I promise I'll do everything I can to get you out. I'll try and raise money as soon as I'm out and I can see people."

"You'd better, it's only fair. I haven't talked."

"I know and I thank you, and if I had the money I'd get us all out of here, I swear."

"All of this is your fault. You ruined my life."

"I'm sorry, I told you a million times I'm sorry. I didn't know this would happen."

"Is there a problem?" Latisha squeezed past Janet and sat on my bed, looking at her through narrowed eyes.

"Latisha, it's cool," I said.

"Okay, so I can talk to you?"

Janet walked off.

"Listen babygirl, I'm gonna miss you, bad. Will you write me?"

"Of course."

"Can I call you?"

"Yes, call me."

"Listen, you know you're my girl, right? I always had your back here."

"Yeah, I know. Thank you so much, girlfriend. You've been my best friend since I got here."

"Then don't forget me."

A CO summoned me a few hours later. When I was brought into the now familiar meeting room, there sat Bernie, my jeweler. He owned a shop on Main Street I frequented often while buying gold earrings, chains, and gifts.

"Bernie, what are you doing here?"

"I'm your bondsman, kid. Your man gave me ten grand and I'm writing you the bond for the rest. You gotta promise me you won't skip."

"Bernie, I swear, I won't."

"Okay. Sign here." He pushed a paper towards me, which I signed without reading.

He studied my face. "You look like shit. What have they been doing to you here?"

"Nothing, I just don't have any makeup on."

"Well, when you're out come and see me. If you need money, I can help you out. You can sell me some of your jewelry. I buy gold by the ounce."

I was released from custody gradually. I went through a series of waiting rooms where I signed endless papers. In the last room, I was given everything I was wearing the night I got busted, along with my purse. I ducked into a bathroom to put on makeup for the first time in months. It was too hot to wear my leathers. When they opened the final cell door, the COs wished me luck and I thanked them without turning around. Every step I took outside the bars was strange, as if I'd forgotten how to walk. I pushed open the door to the parking lot and breathed fresh outside air for the first time in months. I immediately sat down on the curb, having no idea how I was getting home.

"Sissy?" I looked up and there was Seely, waiting with a taxi.

"How did you manage this?" I hugged her tightly as she burst into tears.

"How do you think?"

We rode back to Southbridge. The sun looked brighter than I remembered and the tiny green leaves on the trees were the most beautiful things I'd ever seen.

When we got to my apartment, Seely pulled a crumpled hundred-dollar bill from the pocket of her jeans and paid the driver. She took my bag and carried it up the stairs to my apartment. I trailed behind, gripping the banister while I walked up a set of stairs for the first time in months. I was so unsteady on my feet, I felt like I was ninety years old.

We decided to order take out. I picked up the phone, went to dial, and broke down. I dropped the phone on the floor. We were not allowed to dial the phone in jail. When we made a call, the COs dialed then handed us the receiver through the bars.

Seely came over and hugged me. "What's wrong?"

"Nothing, Seely, will you call for me? And call Nikki, see if she can come over."

I stayed in my apartment the next few days, mainly hanging out with Nikki and having meltdowns. Everything from taking a shower to smoking a joint would send me into a tizzy. Finally, Nik had to go to Florida, to bring back a ki.

I was alone in my apartment for the first time that evening. Around 10 p.m., I heard a knock. I walked towards the door, wondering how people always seemed to get into my building even though the main door was supposed to be locked.

"Who is it?"

"It's your lover, puta, open the door." It was the unmistakable voice of Carlos.

"I really don't want company right now, can we talk tomorrow?"

"Sure," he said.

I walked away from the door and continued down the long hall towards my bedroom. I heard a loud crash. I turned around to see Carlos standing there. He had kicked the door in, splitting the wood of the doorjamb. I ran to my bedroom and jumped across my bed, reaching for my nightstand where I kept a hunting knife. As I pulled the drawer open, Carlos jumped on top of me and the drawer went crashing to the ground. He kneeled over me and slapped me hard in the face.

"Is that any way to treat your pimp?"

"Get off me fucker, what do you want?"

"You owe me fifteen grand, perra, it's your fault the pigs took my stuff."

"Why is it my fault?"

"Don't talk back!"

He bit my shoulder, and blood started to run down my arm.

"You're a fucking animal, maricón!"

We started to wrestle, and he grabbed my hair, pulling me to the floor.

"Get off of me!" I kicked him and stood up, preparing to run. He jumped up and pushed me against the wall, holding me by the throat. He squeezed tighter as I struggled. Finally, I stood still and just as he relaxed his grip slightly, I slapped him so hard on his left cheek my hand stung. He let go of me and touched his face.

"Ow! Ow! You fucking crazy bitch, that hurt!"

He stumbled down the hall towards the front door. I ran to the other side of my room and grabbed my hunting knife off the floor, pulling it from its sheath. I returned to the door of my bedroom, pointing the knife at him.

He laughed with his signature loony howl. "Whatcha gonna do with that, estúpida? I'm leaving; you're acting totally crazy. I'll be back in a few with a gun to kill you with, unless you get my money. I'll give you a couple of days. See some of your friends, see if they can help you out."

I heard him stomp down the stairs. I went to my bedroom window and watched him walk down the street. I couldn't call the police, he'd be out in an hour and then he would kill me for sure. He'd been in and out of the police station at least ten times in the past year, including the night I was busted. Vandalism, illegal firearms, harassment, I watched in disbelief as he was repeatedly set free. He was a ticking bomb, but he had to get caught doing something really serious to be put away again. So the cops kept letting him go, waiting for him to do something worse.

I got a bottle of vodka and took it to bed with me. I drank until I passed out.

The next day, I paged Tyrone six times before he called me back.

"Ty, what's up?" I said when he finally called.

"Nothing, how are you?"

"I'm okay, but I need to talk to you. Can you come over?"

"Um, no can do, sorry baby."

"But I need to speak to you as soon as possible."

"Why don't we meet tonight at Hector's, say ten o'clock?"

"Can't you just come here?"

"No, I'll explain later. Just meet me at Hector's."

I walked into Hector's a little before ten and saw Javon sitting at the bar. He was a regular fixture here, so I had hoped I might see him. I went and sat next to him. He had probably been on the same stool since noon.

"Javon, I'm so sorry about Jamal." I hugged him tightly.

"Thanks girl. When did you get out?"

"Just a few days ago, I'm out on bail. Listen, what the hell happened? My sister said your house was quarantined, what happened to Jamal?"

"Oh, they took that quarantine thing away, it was a mistake. He got some virus that's been killin' people. They said we all have it."

"It's contagious?"

"Nah, not like a cold or anything. The docs said we got it from sharing needles."

"Are you gonna be okay? What's gonna happen to you?"

"No one knows. I might die too. I mean, I feel okay, but listen, I gotta talk to you, do you have time?" His face looked haggard with deep worry lines.

Just then I saw Tyrone walk in, his eyes searching the room for me.

"Javon, I gotta meet someone, we'll talk after, okay? I love you." I kissed him and jumped off my barstool, walking towards Tyrone.

"Hey Ty," I gave him a tight hug, but he barely squeezed me back.

"Chica, let's sit at a table."

We sat at a tiny round table in the back under the shadow of the jukebox.

"Listen, my bosses don't want me talking to you. I'm in trouble if they find out I was with you."

"What? Why? Tyrone, I swear, I never said a word. That's why they cooled me for the last three months at county. But now I'm out on bail."

"And you're hot. You don't think the feds are watching you? Christ, the fucking DEA busted you. And everyone is saying that you talked."

"No way, I didn't. I wouldn't be here right now if I did."

"Babygirl, I believe you, I do. But I still can't be hanging around you, okay? It's not my choice."

I fiddled with the thick, gold link bracelet he always wore. "Tyrone, Carlos says he's gonna kill me. He already broke into my house. I had to get a guy over today to repair my front door and add new locks and everything. He's threatening to shoot me and you know he's nuts. Please, I need protection. Ty, I'm desperate."

"Sorry, I am, really, I just can't."

"But you always said you wanted to be with me … I thought we had something."

"We might have, if you'd left that bastard when I asked you to. You loved him, not me, and now you want me to help you?"

"I cared about you, I did. Things were just complicated. I'll do whatever you say now, whatever you want, I swear. I don't want to be killed, please, I'm begging you."

He placed his hand on the back of my head and pulled me close, until our foreheads touched. He spoke in a low voice. "Baby, baby … I can't help you now. I gotta go, I can't even be seen with you. I'm sorry, but you gotta lose my number." He kissed me then got up and walked out.

I returned to the bar. Javon hadn't moved from his stool. Tears rolled down my face and I let them fall. I ordered a shot of peach schnapps and ordered a refill for Javon. "Make me a tab, hey Hector?" I said to the owner who was tending bar. I had no cash to spend. He nodded in accord.

"You okay, honey?" Javon slurred his words.

"No, I'm not."

He put an arm around my shoulder. "You're gonna be okay. You'll be okay, alright? And you gotta know I'm really sorry."

"It's cool Javon."

"No, no it ain't. And I'm not gonna die without telling you. Listen, you gotta know."

"I gotta know what?" I ordered another shot.

He hung his drunken head. Then, he looked up at me with tears on his cheeks. "You can't trust no one, girl, no-fucking-body."

"I already know that, Von."

"I dropped dime on you that night. I'm sorry … I'm really sorry. I swear, I love you, I fucking love you. You gotta forgive me."

"What are you talking about?" I stroked his head, "Javon, you're drunk, you didn't do anything to me."

"I did, baby, I did, and you gotta forgive me, you gotta. That night, you know, when you went down. Armando paid me to make the call to say when you'd be there."

I stood up so fast my barstool toppled to the floor. Everyone looked at me. I ran outside and threw up on the sidewalk. Then, I started to walk.

I walked around the city feeling the warm summer air, thoughts rushing through my head so fast I felt dizzy. I knew Armando had an inside connection in the police, the crooked cop we called Joe. I had watched him plot against his competitors. I saw him take people down with the law, but they were pimps and junkies who we looked down on, who were our competitors. Armando could not have done this to me; he said I was his right hand! But why would Javon say that?

I kept recalling how desperately Armando begged me to go with him that night at La Casa, just hours before my arrest.

Twenty-Nine

July 1986
Age 18

I never said anything to Armando about what Javon told me. I knew he'd insist it was absurd and maybe even harm Javon. I was learning to keep quiet and bide my time. Rumors were swirling everywhere. When I showed up at The Disco Lounge, my friends treated me differently. They tried to hide it, but it was obvious. I had fallen from grace.

Armando gave me a little money to tide me over. He also fronted me some coke. I was now dealing grams. I was as low on the totem pole as you could go. But I still needed to survive. Some of my old high school friends were willing to buy from me.

Carlos continued to threaten me, mostly over the phone. He hadn't been back to my apartment since the night he broke in. One day, though, he called me repeatedly, threatening to come to my house if I didn't go to his to discuss our "little problem." So I agreed.

I stood in Carlos' living room with a large white purse slung over my shoulder, resting on my hip. I started explaining that I was back in the biz, and I'd be able to pay him as soon as I got things running.

Sitting on the wooden floor of his empty living room, snorting lines and weighing out tiny packets of coke, he looked up at me and grinned. He was wearing his signature red velvet sweat suit, even though it was hot as hell outside. A bunch of gold chains hung from his thick neck, flashing from under the collar of his jacket. He smeared some cocaine on his gums and smacked his lips. Then, he quickly pulled a 9mm handgun out of his velvet pocket, pointed it directly at me and pulled the trigger three times. The explosions were deafening. Three bullets pocked the plaster wall inches from me.

"Shut up," he snarled.

"You could've just killed me," I cried, my body still reeling from the loud explosions.

"If I wanted to hit you I would have."

I opened my purse to get my keys and leave. As I felt for them, I touched something wet. It turned out to be blue ink. A pen exploded, I thought, but as I began to examine my bag, I found six holes, three in front, three in back. All three bullets had passed through my purse while it rested on my hip.

"You ruined my purse, maricón and those bullets could have hit my stomach! You can't treat me like this, it's not my fault we got busted, I'm facing life in prison, you weren't even in the raid."

"Kickin' flavor—I like it. Come're."

"No, fuck you!"

"Come on. I'll pay you."

"I'm no fucking hooker, pendejo."

"Nope. But you will be, you gotta do what I say, you're my bitch now. I own you. You're gonna be my girlfriend, and you're gonna turn tricks and give me the money. Then, I'll be a pimp."

"No fucking way, you're out of your mind. You can just kill me right now." I sat down on the floor and started to cry.

"Come on now, putaña, I'm not gonna kill you now. The suspense is too much fun. Just tell people I'm your man, that's all, you know you need protection."

"I need protection from you."

"Hey, get real, estúpida, I'm not your only enemy. Just do this one thing I ask, and I'll let you pay me off with your little gram business."

"Loco cabrón!"

I went to the bathroom and got toilet paper to dry my face. I walked back into the living room. Carlos was still sitting on the floor. I stood by the window. We were on the fourth floor; I could see the sidewalk below. I contemplated jumping. I opened the window and leaned out, breathing in the sticky air.

I left Carlos' shaking, barely able to drive. I went back to my apartment and blasted Wham! while I got dressed up. I still went out dancing most nights at The Disco Lounge, though nothing felt the same. I was lost.

One night, as I crossed the parking lot of The Lounge, a squad car pulled in front of me, blocking my path.

"Hey Lady." It was Sergeant Conroy. "I heard you were out, you look great."

I leaned in the window of his car. "Yeah, Sarge, I'm out."

"I thought I might find you here."

"Are you serious? You're looking for me?"

"Well, I drive through from time to time is all, but I'm always hoping I'll see you."

"I thought you were confined to your desk."

"Sometimes police business gets me out."

There was another officer in the car who stayed quiet, but he smiled at me.

"Listen, Carl, it was good to see you, but I gotta go."

"I wanted to ask if you'd want to go out one night, you know, to dinner or something?"

"Are you kidding? I'm out on bail, you can't be hanging out with me."

I thought of the five grams of coke in my purse and I wondered if he had any idea I was still dealing.

"Come on, at least gimme your number." He handed me a small notepad and pen. I jotted my phone number down. "I really gotta go now."

"I'll call you." He flashed me a wide, impish grin and drove off.

I continued walking towards The Lounge. Conner was working the door. He gestured for me to come to the front of the line and held his arm out, motioning for me to go inside. When I walked past him he said, "Friends with the cops now?"

"Not friends like we were, Conner."

"Shhh."

"I know, you'd never want Armando to know about that, especially now that you work with him."

"Alright, just please be quiet."

That was the only thing I had left. Blackmail. People who had crossed Armando by fooling around with me were afraid to openly snub me. I'd lost my customers, my status, my protection, my money, and my friends. I'd lost everything. And any day now, I might lose my life.

Thirty

"Nik, I'm so fucking scared I'm gonna go to prison. Mateo and Janet are still in jail."

"I know, girl, it's fucked up." Nikki sat on my bed, cutting up lines on a mirror for us to snort. I held a bottle of Champagne she had brought over. Armando gave it to her when she had brought back his latest ki. She was now making a couple of runs a month, and she was making good money. She still hung out with me a lot. She and Seely were my only friends.

"Nikki, is … is he with anyone?"

"Girlfriend, you don't want to go there."

"I just need to know."

"Take a hit off that Champagne." I did as she told me. "He's with Colleen, but it's not like you guys. She's totally lying to her man, and she's not running his shit like you were."

"Well, I did catch them fooling around, when he and I first got together."

"Just forget him, girlfriend, he's an asshole. He's always got hookers over his place, and they're really young. You don't need that shit."

"Yeah, yeah, you're right."

But the thought of him with Colleen still cut me.

"You know, Nik, Javon says Armando dropped dime on me."

"No way, no way girl. Why would he do that?"

"I had already paid him for the stuff. And now Carlos wants to kill me. Think how perfect it would be for him if Carlos offed me. I know a lot."

"Yeah, but you'd never talk to the pigs."

"No, I wouldn't. But that's only because I follow a code of honor, and what does he know about that?"

My lawyer's office called me in for an appointment. When I went, I was brought into the office of a stranger.

"Who are you?"

He stood up and held out his hand to me, "I'm Joseph Sims, David's partner. He turned your case over to me."

"Why?"

"Sit down, please."

I sat and he returned to his chair. "I have an in at the county with probation. I got the head of probation to agree to interview you, in fact, she's gonna interview Janet, too. But Janet is an adult. Your advantage is being underage. I think I can get you youthful offender status. David asked me to take your case because I specialized in that before I joined this firm."

"Okay, cool, thanks."

"But listen, I need to talk to you and it has to stay between us. It's serious."

"Okay, it will stay here. Believe me, Joseph, I'm keeping my mouth shut these days. I don't trust anyone."

"And you shouldn't. Look, I'm your lawyer, I'm looking out for you and you alone, do you get what I'm saying?"

"I think so."

"You need to get a job, right now. I don't care if you work flipping burgers, but you need to have a job when we go to court. And you need to quit dealing. I know you're still in the game. I'll be honest; you're going to have to plead guilty. If you go to trial you'll spend the next twenty-five years in prison, guaranteed. Plead guilty and you'll only serve three, maybe even probation if you're very lucky."

"Are you serious? I thought I was going to get off."

"No way. And your friends—they're not your friends. If I were you I'd move away after this. You're in danger, and you're hanging out with some bad people. Now, I know this firm gets lots of money from people like your friends, and that's our job, to defend them. But I couldn't sleep at night if I let a kid go to the sharks."

"Joseph, I don't know what you are talking about." Actually, I knew what he was saying was true, but I just couldn't face it. Where would I go?

"I know, just do what I tell you. Quit dealing, if the cops catch you with so much as a gram you're going down. They still want you. Get a job, take this plea bargain, and don't trust anyone. You have no friends right now, except me."

I left his office confused and scared. He was cryptic, but I thought he was saying Armando was out to harm me in some way. And he said I might do three years. Three fucking years! I was terrified of prison, but rolling on Armando still never crossed my mind as an option.

I called Zack. "Daddy, you gotta get me a job. A real job."

"Sure dolly, I'll get you one right away. How about in the lab?"

"Whatever."

And before I knew it, I was getting up at 5 a.m. Monday through Friday, driving an hour to sift dirt in the lab at the construction company my father had worked at the past twenty years. My paycheck was a joke. I worked forty hours for the same amount we once paid for a single limo ride. I picked up a few customers at work, which was cool, but I was still totally humiliated. I once got regular manicures. Now, my hands were literally in dirt all day long.

I still partied at The Lounge, drinking more than ever. Sometimes I went to work without even sleeping and still drunk. I hawked grams and I often gave Carlos all the money in my purse when he would show up at random and shake me down.

Late in September, I was on the dance floor when Conner and another bouncer named Jack came to find me.

"You gotta come outside. Carlos is freaking out in the parking lot, saying he has to see you. We'll go with you."

I followed them out to find Carlos standing next to his car in a pair of white silk pajamas. Before I could speak he hit me in the mouth, and my lip started to bleed.

"I've had it with you perra! You've given me a lousy two grand and your partying every night. You're coming with me."

He took my arm and began pulling me towards the car. Conner and Jack grabbed me and pulled me back.

Carlos yelled at them, "Get your hands off my bitch!"

"Just calm down," said Conner, but both bouncers looked frightened, even though they were each at least twice the size of Carlos.

Carlos went into his car and came out waving a gun. "Now, are you two gonna leave, or do I have to shoot you both too?"

Everyone stood still for what felt like hours. I pressed my hand to my throbbing lip. Then, Conner said, "Look, I'm sorry, we can't get involved."

I latched onto his sleeve. "What do you mean? Don't leave me."

He pulled his arm free. "It'll be alright. You two just talk it out."

240

"Talk? He's gonna kill me."

"I'm sorry." Conner turned and Jack followed him back inside the nightclub.

"So much for your bodyguards." Carlos howled with laughter. He shoved me to the ground and stood over me, pointing the 9mm at me. After a few minutes he lowered the gun and said, "I'm not gonna kill you here, too many witnesses. I'll come and get you at your house." He walked back to his tan Cadillac Seville, got in, and drove off.

I went back into The Lounge and started screaming at Conner. "You fucking coward, how could you leave me like that?"

"What was I supposed to do? He had a gun. And I can't call the cops, this place is full of coke, they'd shut us down."

I punched him hard as I could on the arm. "I hate you!"

I went to the ladies room and locked myself in a stall, where I closed the lid to the toilet, sat down, and started to cry. Conner sent Melissa in to find me.

She knocked on the stall door. "Girlfriend, are you ok?"

"I'm fine, tell your boy I'm just fucking fine."

"Well, let me sit with you."

I came out of the stall and we sat in the lounge part of the bathroom snorting coke from my bullet.

"What are you going to do now?" Melissa asked.

"I'm going to go home and let him come kill me. What else can I do?"

Melissa was sweet. She put her hand on mine. "I'm sorry for you girl. It's not fair … the way things are."

Thirty-One

I decided to move. Since Carlos had not come and killed me yet, I figured I might as well take some action to escape being gunned down. I didn't want to live, but I was also terrified of death, and especially of being murdered.

I rented a small house on the edge of town. It was behind another house, totally hidden from the street. It had a backyard with some nice trees, and a private driveway so my car wouldn't be parked on the road. I thought maybe Carlos wouldn't be able to find me here. I had no idea how long I'd be there. My sentencing was on November 25.

One night I was home alone, packing boxes, and I heard sirens that sounded like they were right outside my house. I looked out the windows but didn't see anything. Since sirens were common in my neighborhood, I didn't think much more about it.

I awoke the next morning to the shrilling of my doorbell. It was Nikki.

"Chica, look." She threw the local paper on my kitchen table. "Carlos killed somebody last night, just around the corner from here."

We read the story. He was walking, and he got into an argument on the street with a young Puerto Rican man. He pulled out a gun and shot him three times. Then, he ran away. He would never have been caught, there were no witnesses and Carlos didn't even know the guy, he was just some random junkie. But Carlos, on his endless quest to get back to prison, turned up at the hospital to check on the guy, who was already dead. The police started questioning him and they decided to search him. He had the murder weapon in his pocket.

He had only been out of prison thirteen months.

"Girl, it's over. You don't even need to move." Nikki hugged me tightly.

"I'm still gonna move, what if they let that fucker out on bail?"

"No way, girl, he's gonna do life for this. You're safe now."

"Nik, he must've been walking here. That guy he killed took my bullet."

A few days later the phone calls started.

"Hey putaña, you miss me?"

"Carlos? How are you using the phone, I thought you were in jail?"

"Yeah, but I'm a trustee. I'm cleaning the guard's office and there's a phone on the desk."

I hung up on him. Over the next week he called at least a dozen times, mostly leaving messages on my machine. "I'm gonna count the days until I get out and come kill you, I don't care if it takes twenty years."

Once, I picked up and tried to reason with him. "Carlos, why do you want to kill me? I never did anything to you."

"You fucked up my life by telling that maricón boyfriend of yours about us. I lost my stuff because of your big mouth. You gotta pay, perra. See you in twenty."

244

When I moved, I got a new number, so I never heard from Carlos again. Within the month he plead guilty and was sentenced to twenty-five years to life in prison.

I was in my new house less than a week when I got a call from Nikki. Her voice sounded low.

"Nikki, what's up? Are you alright?"

"No, I'm not." She was crying softly, something I'd never heard before.

"What's wrong, girlfriend?"

"I'm in jail, in Florida. The feds got me. I was getting on the plane. I don't know what to do, they're talking fifty years."

"What about bail? Did they set bail?"

"No, they say they don't have to. It's totally different when it's federal. What am I gonna do? My mom needs me, I could be here forever." She sobbed into the phone.

"Nikki, listen, I love you, it's gonna be alright. I'll go see your mom, she knows me. And I'll talk to whoever else I can." I meant that I'd talk to Armando, but I couldn't even hint at him. We were definitely talking on a tapped line.

"They're saying I gotta go."

"Nikki, listen, call me. Call as much as you can. I'm here."

"Okay." Her voice sounded flat and distant.

I raced out the door, drove to Armando's, and rang his doorbell frantically.

He opened the door. "Chica, what's wrong? Um, *entra*." He stepped aside and I walked into the living room. Colleen sat on the sofa, decked out with a drink in her hand. She nodded at me but said nothing.

"We were just going to dinner, ah, you can come with —"

"No, I need to talk to you. Privately."

"Sí, sí. Come into the kitchen."

I followed him to the kitchen and we both sat at the wobbly table. All the money he had and he still owned nothing but junk for furniture.

"Chica, are you okay?"

"Save your bullshit Armando, you don't care about me. I'm here because the feds got Nikki."

"Qué? No, no *es posible.*"

"They've had her since this morning."

"*Madona*! The kilo ... they have got my ki?"

"They've got it and they're talking about her doing fifty years. Fifty years!"

He looked stricken. "I just lost twenty grand."

"Fuck your money, maricón!"

"Sí, sí, I'm sorry, I just ... I'll get her a lawyer. I'll call my people in Miami."

"I gotta go, I gotta tell her mother."

He took out his wallet and handed me three hundred dollar bills. "Here, give this to her madre, sí? Oh, and she won't talk, *correcto*? Did you tell her not to?"

"She knows not to. We all do."

Thirty-Two

I had left my spacious ritzy apartment and moved to a tiny house. My fancy furniture looked out of place among the stained carpets and peeling wallpaper. I stayed home most nights, hanging out with a handful of high school friends who came over to drink cheap beer, smoke joints, and snort coke. I partied with them, hoping for numbness that might quell the constant, nagging fear of prison. I spent less and less time at The Lounge, where I had become an outcast.

Now a small time gram dealer, I bought a fake soda can weighted to feel like it was full. The top screwed open revealing a hollow chamber made to hide valuables. I kept grams of coke inside, hiding it under my front porch. My logic was that if I were raided again the stuff wouldn't be in my house, so no one could prove it was mine.

One night some friends were at my house sniffing lines, when they began talking about people in the trees.

"What the fuck are you wastoids talking about?" I laughed at them.

"I'm telling you, there are guys up in the trees behind your house," my friend Drew said.

"Yeah, I saw them too," Jeff chimed in.

"You guys are crazy."

I went outside, into the dark of my backyard, and studied the trees. There was no one there. I determined the coke had simply made these guys so paranoid, they were seeing things. It became a joke among my friends, those watchers up in the trees.

Mid-month, my lawyer Joseph called me in to his office to coach me for my probation interview.

"Let's see. Can you say you have a drug problem?"

"Well, I really don't, but I sure as hell have an alcohol one."

"Say you're an alcoholic and you want treatment. Is anyone in your family alcoholic?"

"All of them."

"Good. I mean, for your case. What about your family? Tell me about them."

When I told him the story of how I ended up living alone at fifteen, he looked sympathetic.

"Wow, that's some story you have. I'm sorry you've had it so rough. Just make sure you tell the probation officer everything you told me."

I went to my appointment at probation two weeks before my sentencing. I met with the head of the department, a social worker named Susan. Our interview lasted three hours. I told her my parents were married three times each, and that my mother left Seely and me before we could finish high school.

"What did you want to do after high school?"

"I wanted to go to college for English."

"Do you like to read?"

"Oh, I love books, they're my life." I pulled a copy of The Scarlet Letter out of my purse. "This is what I'm reading now."

Her face was soft and when she saw the book, her eyes misty. I thought she was a sucker.

"You said you're an alcoholic. When did you start drinking?"

"When I was twelve."

"Where was your mother?"

"Out having affairs on her second husband."

"Do you drink everyday?"

"Yes."

"Do you want to stop?"

"Yes, I do, I want to, but it's the only thing that kills the pain."

"What pain?"

"The pain of being alive."

The next two weeks were hell. I missed Nikki terribly; her stalwart eyes and soothing manor had preserved me many times. I missed Tommy and Colleen and Conner, but I also hated them. And despite everything, I even missed Armando. But most of all, I missed the glamorous life; the visceral power of a somewhat bottomless purse, and the feeling of invincibility that came with it. I missed being a cocaine queen. Now, I'd be lucky to simply escape prison.

The day of my sentencing arrived. I had stayed up all night unable to sleep, pacing my house, wondering if I'd get to come back home. I looked for incriminating things to dispose of, in case someone else packed up my house.

Early morning I showered and dressed for court. I wore the conservative black suit my lawyer suggested. I drove myself to the county courthouse almost an hour away. A hundred times I thought of turning the car towards Florida, of running. But life on the run scared me. I'd never be able to come back to New York, or to see Zack or Seely.

When I got to court, I saw Janet and Mateo sitting in the front, shackled. Neither had ever made bail, both had been in jail these past ten months.

The wooden seats in the court were long, like church pews. When I went to sit, I saw Zack and Leona sitting with Joan and Seely. I sat next to Seely.

"Seel, what are those losers doing here?"

She started crying and put her arms around me. "Sissy, I don't want you to go, you can't go. The prison is hours away … I won't be able to hitchhike there."

"It's okay," I said. I held her tightly, "If I go, I promise I'll write you everyday. And I'll be out in three."

"Three years! No, sis, no."

Seely wept into my hair. Joan glared at me from behind Seely's head.

"Why are you even here?" I asked her.

"'Cause I brought your sister. Look how upset she is. I'm telling ya, you're rotten to the core. I always said you was."

Zack leaned over Leona to hush my mother. "This isn't the time for this shit, everyone just try and get along. Joan, our daughter is in serious trouble!"

"Well, whose fucking fault is that? It sure ain't mine!"

My lawyer was nowhere to be seen. I started getting nervous. Where the hell was he? Then, in walked Colleen and Melissa. Colleen hugged me tightly, letting out a sob. Melissa kissed my cheek. Colleen sat down next to me, and held my hand tightly.

Melissa leaned over, offering Seely and Colleen tissues. She said, "Conner sends his love. He'd be here, except, well, you know, you have to sign in and—"

"It's okay, I understand."

"Girl, I'm really sorry. I don't want you to go away, I'm praying for you."

"Thanks, Melissa, thanks for coming."

"I'm happy to be here, plus, she's kinda drunk and she needed a driver."

"I'm not fucking drunk," said Colleen. Then she hiccupped and we all cracked up.

The judge came in and sat on a high podium in a big black leather chair. He called Mateo first. All three of us had struck an agreement to plead guilty to lesser charges.

"You are charged with a class C felony of possession, how do you plead?"

"Guilty, your honor."

"You are charged with a class C felony of intent to distribute, how do you plead?"

"Guilty, your honor."

"You are charged with a class E felony of possession of drug packaging equipment, how do you plead?"

"Guilty, your honor."

"You are charged with a class A misdemeanor of possession of paraphernalia, how do you plead?"

"Guilty, your honor."

The courtroom was silent as the judge sat scratching notes on his papers.

"This court hereby sentences you to no less than three years and no more than ten years in state prison."

Seely and Colleen both resumed weeping while the CO standing near Mateo took him away.

Next, Janet was called. All the same charges were listed, all the same guilty pleas entered. She was sentenced identically. As the CO led her away, she looked to the back of the courtroom at us, her face a mix of contempt and fear. I was filled with guilt over her fate, and fear of what was coming for me.

I saw my lawyer walk in with Susan, the probation officer who had interviewed me, and sit at a table in front of the courtroom. He asked the judge if he could approach the bench and then stepped forward, speaking privately to the judge. He returned to his seat and my name was promptly called. I stood up with legs of jelly. Seely clung to my sleeve, forcing me to pry myself loose. I handed her my purse. "Here, Seely, hold this and give Daddy my car keys if they take me away."

The judge called my name again impatiently, and I walked forward and stood before him. He read out the identical charges once more, and I plead guilty to each, as my codefendants had done.

"Young lady, are you aware of the seriousness of the charges you've just plead guilty too?"

"Yes, your honor."

"Ms. Ryder has recommended you to this court for probation in lieu of prison but this court is skeptical. Mr. Sims tells me you are working?"

"Yes, your honor, I am."

"What do you do?"

"I ... I work in a lab, in construction."

"And what do you do there."

"Um, I sift rock through screens."

"Sift rock? For what purpose?"

"Well, um, to determine the quality of the soil at a construction site."

"And why is this important?"

"It's needed to know the type of concrete that must be used for the foundation, your honor." My voice was shaking. I felt like I was in a horrible game show where you might lose your life. And I felt tiny before the omnipotent judge high up above me.

"I am asking these questions to determine if you really are working. Anyone can produce a piece of paper that says they're employed."

"I really am working, your honor. I get up 5 a.m. every day and drive an hour. And I really love my job."

The judge snorted. The room remained silent while he scratched away again with his pen.

"I have decided I am going to go with the recommendation of Ms. Ryder and sentence you to time served plus five years probation, only because you are a minor, but let me tell you something right now. If you come into this court on even one violation, no matter how small, I will revoke your probation and sentence you to a full ten-year term in state prison. Do you understand me?"

"Yes, your honor."

"Then you are free to go."

I turned away and began walking in a daze, nearly tripping over my own feet. I was stunned. Joseph came from behind the table and hugged me saying in my ear, "Listen to the judge, don't fuck it up, he means it. And congratulations."

"Thank you, thank you so much." Tears of relief flowed as I shook the hand of Susan Ryder then stumbled through the half gate that separated the front part of the courtroom from the larger galley. Seely, Colleen and Melissa ran up to me. Everyone hugged me in a big huddle, all of us crying and laughing until the judge pounded his gavel ordering us to be quiet. We rushed back to our seats and gathered up our coats. Zack hugged and kissed me, Joan ignored me, but I didn't see Leona.

We all left the courtroom, walking through double doors into a large hallway. Everyone started speaking at once. I said that we should all go see Janet and Mateo in prison. We talked of going for lunch first. We headed for the front doors of the county building. I had one arm around Seely and one around Colleen, and then, someone pulled on my shoulder from behind. I turned to see Joseph.

"Joseph, do you want to come out to eat with us?"

"No, listen, you need to come upstairs to probation immediately. It's an emergency."

I told everyone to wait.

We jogged up the marble staircase to the office door of Ms. Ryder. I followed Joseph into Susan's office, where I saw Leona sitting on a chair in front of her desk.

"What's going on?"

"Sit down," said Susan, and I sat, making sure there was a chair between Leona and me.

"Your stepmother is asking that your probation be revoked, she says you're still dealing drugs."

I looked at Leona. "You lying cunt, you don't even know me! You know nothing about my life!"

"Okay, you need to calm down so we can discuss this," said Joseph.

"There's nothing to discuss, she lies, she always has, and she's drunk, look at her! She's slurring her speech! I'll kill her, Joseph, I will."

"Honey, I'm only doing this because I love you and I don't want you getting messed up anymore with drugs. You're like my own daughter, you know that."

"Joseph, can you go get my father? He'll clear this up."

Joseph left. Leona continued to talk and Susan listened, shaking her head from time to time. Joseph returned with my father, who came behind me and put a comforting hand on my shoulder.

He looked confused at first, and then furious. He stared at Leona and said, "What's going on here?"

Susan answered him. "Well, you see, your wife says your daughter is still dealing drugs. Do you believe that?"

"Absolutely not! My daughter works very hard at my company, she comes in every day, on time. I visit her at her apartment weekly and she is not dealing."

"Why would your wife lie?"

My father's eyes were aflame as he continued to look at Leona. "My wife has a problem with lying, and with drinking. She always been jealous of both my kids from my first marriage and she takes it out on them."

"Okay, okay. I would like to speak to my probationer alone for a few minutes."

After the room emptied Susan reached her hand across the desk and gestured for mine. I put my hand in hers while I sat speechless and crying.

"So that's them, huh?"

"Yup."

"Well, all your stepmother did was strengthen my conviction that you deserve a second chance. She's exactly as you described. And she'll never get an audience with me again, I promise."

Later that night, after the longest day of my life, a few of my friends came over to drink champagne with me. We all got extremely drunk. Seely threw up on herself, most of it landing on her feet. I washed her shoes and socks in the bathroom sink, giving her a pair of my nylons to wear home under her damp sneakers. I called her boyfriend to come pick her up and then I hung her wet socks over the shower rod to dry, not knowing they would become part of a kind of shrine, not knowing we would never party together again.

Thirty-Three

ICU: Abbreviation for Intensive Care Unit; a large room where patients are kept in curtained rooms in a circle around the nurses' station, so they can be watched continually.

One week after my sentencing, I was watching Hill Street Blues when the phone rang. I ignored it, but the person hung up on my machine and immediately called again. I ran to the phone thinking maybe it was Nikki, even though it was late for her to be allowed to use the phone from jail.

A woman asked for me. Then she said, "Listen, I have some bad news. Can you sit down?"

"Who is this?"

"My name is Debbie, I'm a nurse at Brookfield hospital."

"What's wrong? What's happened?"

"Please sit down first"

I hastily sat on a kitchen chair. "Okay, I'm sitting, please tell me what's wrong."

"It's your sister, she's been in an accident—a car accident."

"Is she alive?"

"Yes, she is, but we need you to come here right away. Do you know how to reach your parents?"

"Yes."

"Can you call them? They need to come too."

"Is she going to be alright?"

"The doctor will answer all your questions when you get here. And listen, drive slow, the roads are icy out there."

I quickly called both of my parents in succession. I was bawling so much I was mostly unintelligible.

Contrary to the nurse's advice I punched my Camaro, driving close to 90mph the entire way to the hospital. My head raced with questions. Why wouldn't the nurse explain more about her condition? Who was Seely with, and why did they have my phone number?

I ran through the sliding glass doors towards the admittance counter, but before I reached the clerk to ask for Seely, Armando appeared. He looked stricken, and his cheek had a bloody scratch. I ran up to him and began punching him while screaming curses in Spanish. He held his arms over his face trying to protect himself from the blows.

"I told you this would happen, you mother fucking bastard! What did you do to Seely?"

He took my beating until security guards came and pulled me off him. His voice quivered when he finally spoke. "Mira, you should speak to the doctor. They won't tell me anything. I am not family."

I went over to the counter and continued my tirade, rudely demanding to talk to a doctor. The young receptionist froze in fear. A nurse came out from behind a glass wall and told me to calm down.

258

"I know you're upset, but you can't act like this. We'll talk to Seely's parents when they get here, they're coming, right?"

"I don't fucking know! They threw us on the street years ago, we have no parents, now you get me the fucking doctor or I'll call the police … I'll sue all of you!"

She walked away and in minutes, a man walked out in bloodstained surgeons' scrubs and latex gloves. He pulled his mask down to talk to me.

"Listen to me, young lady, you need to calm down. This is a hospital, people here are sick and we won't tolerate profanities. I could hear you yelling in the operating room."

"I'm sorry, okay … please, I just need someone to tell me how my sister is?"

"She's paralyzed from the neck down, and that's only if she lives. I'm very sorry. I suggest you call a friend to come wait with you; I have to get back to surgery. I'll talk to you after."

I stood frozen in shock. Armando walked over to me, and I slapped his face as hard as I could.

"Stay away from me, estúpido maricón! She's paralyzed, fucking paralyzed! You fucking son of a bitch, you destroyed my sister's life. You should die!"

"But you need to let me explain, por favor. I was taking her and Bonnie to the mall. It wasn't my fault, I swear, I was not going fast. There was ice."

"Nothing is ever your fault! You are pure evil!"

"But I swear to you, the car just went out of control—"

I walked away from Armando towards a bank of phone booths. I stood with a phone in my hand having no idea who to dial. Armando stood a few phones away, so I eavesdropped on him talking to his lawyer. He hung up and walked over to me looking distressed.

"Mira, I'm so sorry, but you can't tell anyone what I said. No one can know I was driving. That was my lawyer and he said—"

I took the phone receiver and hit him with it. He jumped back, out of reach of my cord-bound bludgeon. I ran after him and jumped at him, pulling his hair until he broke free. He ran to a bathroom and locked himself in.

I wandered to an empty waiting room and began to scream and wail so loud I was sure the guards would come for me again, but none did. I don't know how long I continued, but eventually I crumpled over onto a couch, sobbing uncontrollably.

I heard the automatic doors. I looked up and saw Zack. I jumped up and ran into his arms.

"Daddy, daddy, Seely is paralyzed, she's paralyzed and the doctor said she might die."

My father held me tightly in his arms. I cried hard into his flannel shirt. Armando emerged and came back into the waiting area having no idea my father was there. Zack let go of me and ran up to Armando, startling him. I never saw my father look so angry. He stood inches from Armando, staring at him with contempt.

"You? You did this?"

"I'm so sorry, please believe me, I am."

My father clenched his teeth and hissed, "I told you to stay away from my daughters!"

Armando slunk away and disappeared.

Soon my mother appeared. I called Seely's boyfriend and he came with his mother. I asked him why Seely was with Armando, but he said he was at work, and he only knew she was out, he didn't know where or who with. We all sat for hours, the only sound being my occasional sobs. Finally, near dawn, the doctor I'd talked to came and told us that Seely might live, and we could come and see her in the ICU.

"But doctor, will she still be paralyzed?" I said.

"I'm afraid so."

We were ushered into a dimly lit room where the noise of a large machine dominated. My sister's eyes were closed. She was connected to tubes taped to her throat and both arms.

"She's sleeping from the anesthesia," the doctor explained, "that machine is breathing for her because both of her lungs were popped in the accident. The tube coming from her throat is a tracheotomy; it connects her to the breathing machine. We are giving her water, food and medicine through the tubes in her arms." A tiny screen bleeped, echoing her heartbeat.

"Will she live?" It was Joan, speaking for the first time in hours. Tears rolled down her face.

"We don't know. I suggest you stay here, there's a special waiting room for ICU, and we even have a small apartment on this floor, just two rooms. We may be able to get it for you. For now, see if you might have family members bring you overnight bags."

We camped in the plushy special ICU waiting room, sleeping on couches. In the afternoon, Mike's mother went to get his stuff, and Leona came with things for my father. I called Sherry, who was always so affectionate, asking her to retrieve my key and bring me a packed bag. She came a few hours later with my stuff and cookies she had baked.

In the evening, a few state troopers came. They told us that the car was going 85 mph, and that the driver took a sharp right after almost missing a turn causing the vehicle to flip over three times. Everyone was thrown from the car except Seely. No one was wearing seatbelts. Seely broke her neck by hitting the roof of the car, and burst her lungs by crashing into the dashboard. The two thrown were hardly scratched, but Seely almost suffocated on the scene.

"The strangest thing," the trooper said, "is that a doctor was driving behind them on his way to work at the hospital. He specializes in lungs, so he had a hand-operated breathing machine in his car. He got out and saw Seely, and he hooked her up to his machine and hand pumped air into her lungs until the ambulance arrived. It was a miracle."

"Officer," I said, "was the driver breath tested?"

"No ma'am, everyone had been taken to the hospital when we arrived on the scene, since the accident was less than a mile away. The car owner called today and reported Seely as driving."

"The car owner is my ex-boyfriend, and he was here last night when I arrived. He told me he was driving, and I attacked him. You can ask security, they pulled me off him. I was there when he called his lawyer and he was advised to lie, and to say Seely was driving. He asked me to lie about what he told me at first."

"Can you give a sworn statement to that?"

"Yes."

"Are you aware the other occupant gave a sworn statement that Seely was driving?"

"The other occupant is a lying coke whore. You'd find that out if you tested her for drugs. She might even have a record for prostitution."

They took my statement then prepared to leave handing us a card with a phone number. "When Seely wakes up, call us. We want to get a statement from her."

I had no idea if they believed me. Maybe I sounded nuts, or like a jealous ex-girlfriend. I'm sure I looked crazy; I hadn't slept more than two hours in the past twenty-four.

Later that night, the nurse came to get us. She said, "Seely's awake, and she wants to see you all."

We raced to her room. Seely's bed was tilted upwards, as if she was sitting. She smiled brightly at us and made a clucking sound with her tongue.

"Excuse me, nurse, can she talk?"

"It's not easy for her, but she wants to. She knows you all."

I went over to her and kissed her cheek. "I love you, girl, you gotta get better."

She clucked in response. I turned and saw both my parents crying. Mike went over and held her hand. He was crying too. Seely's eyes looked bright and alive. It was clear she knew us. At that moment, I became convinced she would live and I was relieved, but I was also afraid for her. What kind of life could she have now?

The days dragged on while Seely fought to live. I took long walks through the corridors of the hospital until I knew every twist and turn of its many floors. We slept in the waiting room and on cots in the tiny apartment where we took showers. We ate our meals in the hospital cafeteria. I had never before spent so much time with both my parents.

Seely went through many surgeries, some planned, some emergency. We were often awakened in the middle of the night to come keep vigil at her bedside. She kept pulling through. Then, a week had passed and only my father had gone home for short amounts of time.

Leona would come to the hospital drunk and start fights with Zack. One day she stood in front of my father with her arms crossed and said, "How long will this go on? You have other children who need you!"

My father stood up. "My daughter is dying in there, Leona."

"Well, my children need Christmas presents. They're little, they don't understand."

"You think I give a fuck about Christmas?"

I got up and walked past them, purposefully bumping into my stepmother as I went by. They continued to argue but their voices grew distant, as I began one of my walkabouts along the hospital corridors.

I spent most of my days entertaining visitors. Some, like my grandmother, were allowed in with Seely. Others, like my father's friend Peter, came every day, but was not allowed to see her. Visitors are tiring to those struggling to live.

One evening in the second week, I saw a handsome young man walking across the room towards me. It turned out to be Michael, the DEA agent who busted me. He took my hand as if to shake it, but held it for a moment.

"I'm so very sorry for what's happened here."

"Thanks, that's really nice."

"Listen, I want to take you out of here just for a little while. There's a Holiday Inn right next door. Can we go have a drink and talk?"

I left his pager number with my father, who scowled thinking I was going off with some dealer friend. Who else would I know with a pager?

At the bar, we got a table.

"What'll you have?"

"Vodka on the rocks."

He came back with a beer for himself and a ginger ale for me. "You think I'm going to buy a minor booze? Especially one on probation in an alcohol rehab program?"

"Why do you always know everything about me?"

"It's my job. Just like it's my job to know you're still dealing, and bust you again."

"Why? I'm nothing now, you must know that."

"Because a violation could get you ten years, and facing ten years … that could make you talk. I want Armando, I told you, he is the only one I've ever wanted."

"Michael, I mean, Detective Richards, I can't help you, I've told you that."

"You can call me Michael." He took a sip of his beer. His face was stony and serious. "Look at what Armando has put you through. First jail, now your little sister so seriously injured. And your buddy Nikki may never see daylight again. Don't you want him stopped?"

I sipped my soda in silence. I liked him, but my street code of silence prevented me from saying a word. He was a them—a federales.

"I know you're still dealing. Who do you think is up in those trees every night behind your house? It's my guys and me. I know you keep the coke in a soda can in the bushes outside your house. I was gonna bust you, but now with your sister … I just can't. So I'm here, wrecking my case."

"Why?"

"Because, you're different and even though you can't see it, I can. You don't belong in jail, and I can't send you there now that your sister is hurt. She needs you."

He then told me things, like who was going to get busted among my old friends. Naively, I later warned each to try and save them from getting busted. Instead of being grateful, they viewed me with suspicion. Why was I talking to a fed? Michael had tricked me. He was firmly invested in my being thought of as a rat.

Our glasses were empty. "I need to go back," I said.

"Of course, we'll go. But listen to me, I'm pleading with you. Get away. Just move away … disappear … vanish. How will you help Seely while you're in prison, protecting Armando? Your parents aren't good at taking care of healthy children; you know that better than anyone. I read those letters your school counselor wrote to the judge. He said you never had a mother, that you always took care of her emotionally."

"What? Are you a psychologist too?"

"I took some classes in criminal justice college. Just promise me you'll move away. I took your can so your dealing days are done. And if you don't want to help me take a dangerous man off the streets, I'll get him anyway. Eventually."

"Why, I mean, really, why did you wreck your case, for me?"

"I care about you, it's not something you can understand. You're too young."

"You mean you like me?"

"No, not like that. You're just a messed up kid who can do much better, and I know it. You've got a future, unlike those around you."

Whenever I was with Seely I tried to seem cheerful, but it was so hard. I was exhausted from stress and crying. We watched a movie together once, an old Sandy Dennis about a woman who had a year to live.

I went home, just for the night, on day fifteen. The doctor declared Seely stable and told me to go sleep in my own bed. He said I looked exhausted. It was hard to sleep, and when I did, often someone came to shake me awake and bring me to Seely's room so I could be there if she slipped away.

The doctor who sent me home called me at 11 p.m. and said, "I'd like you to come back soon, sometime tonight."

"I thought you said I should get a good night's rest. Is Seely okay?"

"I just think your family needs you, and you should come back. Just grab some clothes, a little food, maybe, and come back."

So I headed back, but I dragged my feet. My family didn't need me—I didn't have a family. The doctor had said she was stable earlier when he sent me home. She could not have gotten worse that fast. Plus, he was so calm on the phone; there was no urgency in his voice.

On the way back to the hospital, I stopped at The Disco Lounge. It was a Monday night, so I knew it would be dead. And, it was late, nearly 1 a.m.

When I walked towards the bar, I saw Armando sitting there. I didn't expect to see him. Since I no longer knew what he drove, I didn't spot

266

his car in the parking lot. He looked glum, sitting there sulking by himself over his Chivas Regal.

I sat a few stools away and ordered a Scotch. Sherry patted my hand silently while she poured my drink. I reached for my wallet and Armando called out, "I've got it."

He got up and came over, sitting on the stool next to me.

"What do you want, pendejo?"

"I just … how is your sister?"

"Paralyzed."

"I know, I just mean … I want her to be okay." His eyes filled with tears.

I tossed my scotch back and ordered another.

"Mira, chica, I know you hate me, but I swear it was an accident." He dabbed at his eyes with a cocktail napkin.

"Everyone knows even crocodiles can cry."

"Qué? What does this mean?"

"It means take your fake tears away from me, cabrón!"

"They are not fake, I promise, I am so sorry."

We sat in silence. I ordered a third drink, downed it and hopped off the barstool.

"Where are you going?"

"To the hospital."

I walked to the end of the bar and kissed Sherry.

"You take care, honey, call me if you need me. I'll come and visit again soon. I love you."

"Love you too, Sher."

Armando was standing behind me but I ignored him and walked out the door towards my car.

"Chica, please, wait." Armando called out walking after me.

"What do you want? I have to go."

"I just want you to believe that I am sorry, I swear I am." Fresh tears rolled down his face.

"Sorry? You're fucking sorry? If you were sorry, you'd take that Glock outta your glove box and blow your brains out. Better yet, blow mine out, just fucking kill me you bastard!" I rushed towards him, and pounded on his chest with my fists. "You no good cabrón! You destroy everyone. You're evil and I hate you!"

He stood with his arms limp at his sides, letting me hit him. I burst into tears and he hugged me, while I held my clenched fists tightly to my chest.

"Just give me your gun, please, let me die."

"I cannot."

"Why? You gotta help me, you owe me."

"Negrita, I love you."

I pulled away from him and staggered towards my car. I got in and held the steering wheel, weeping. Armando knocked on the window. I glared at him through the glass. I started my car, put it in reverse, and floored it. I jammed the shifter into drive and raced out of the parking lot.

When I reached the hospital, I snuck in using all the back ways I knew from my forays. When I walked into the ICU, two night nurses who knew me well stepped out from their tiny station.

"I'm here to see Seely," I said.

The looks on their faces were peculiar, and they were blocking me from Seely's room.

"Didn't you see your family? They're waiting for you in the front room."

Suddenly, I realized what was happening. My sister was dead.

I ran out of there as fast as I could. Down the long hall I saw Mike and my parents and stepparents all stand up in unison and walk towards me. I stopped and pressed my back to the nearest wall, then crumpled to the ground. My legs just gave out. They all crowded around me.

"Just leave me alone, everyone get away from me!"

Zack pulled me to my feet and dragged me to one of the couches.

"Do you want to see her? They kept her here in case you did."

"No, no, daddy, I can't."

Seely was barley seventeen and it was sixteen days since I walked in here and saw Armando, and then a bloodstained doctor, and then Seely with machines keeping her alive. There was a feeling welling up in me, a tidal wave of pain unlike any I'd felt before. My tears fell so rapidly onto my father's shoulder it seemed impossible. He held me tightly as I cried unabated. His soft brown corduroy vest—the one he always wore—had a tear-stained patch of dark all down the front and back. The others sat stiff and silent while I wailed.

When I was spent (at least for the moment) I said, "Okay, I want to see her now."

My father went off and then returned saying she had already been taken to the morgue.

We all got into the elevator. I was standing dangerously close to Joan, who was glaring at me. I held my father tightly around the waist and started to cry again. "Daddy, Joan hates me, she does. She wishes it was me that was dead. She always said Seely was her favorite and I was yours. She thinks this is all my fault and it is, it is!" I was rambling. Joan didn't say a word.

The funeral home where Seely was waked was directly across the street from my grandmother's house. I had watched wakes all my life from her big picture window. Now, I sat at that window and looked out all day, hour after hour. I kept thinking I'd be okay if Seely was there, close by, and I could keep visiting her, even though her body was cold, and her skin felt hard when I touched it.

Armando send a huge wreath of flowers, the card simply said, "From a friend." Zack angrily had the funeral director remove them. And later, when Armando tried to attend one of the viewings, my father raced to the door and chased him back out onto the street.

Thirty-Four

"You know, I always knew she was going to die," my father said as we sat on my sofa smoking a joint one evening.

"What do you mean? How did you know?"

"When you called the night of the accident, I was asleep. I was having a dream that I saw a baby wriggling in a coffin, and people were closing the coffin lid. I ran up to them and said, 'Don't close that lid, that baby is still moving!'

"One of them said, 'That baby won't be moving for long.' Then, the phone woke me up."

"Why didn't you tell me? Maybe I could've been more prepared, I really thought she might live."

"No, I couldn't tell you. I couldn't take away your hope."

Joan and Zack sued Armando for wrongful death. Armando got Bonnie to testify that Seely was driving. It was two live people against one dead. Bonnie was a homeless teen, a street urchin who Armando,

I imagined, bribed with a hundred dollars. The court threw out my parent's suit but Armando's car insurance company gave them an automatic death payment of fifty thousand dollars. They gave me ten thousand, and I promptly quit my job in order to cry fulltime. I hadn't gone to work anyways the entire month of December.

Two weeks after Seely's funeral, I called Zack. "Daddy, I've decided to move away from Southbridge. Can you come and move me?"

"Of course, I'll get a few of my friends to help. Where are you going?"

"'I'm gonna rent an apartment there, so I can see grandma, and you, and the kids more."

"Sweetheart, that's great. The only thing is, well, what about your friends, you know, the ones who went to prison?"

"What do you mean?"

"Well, aren't you going to help them somehow? I don't think it's fair that only you got off."

"I didn't get off, I'm on probation and I have to do stupid drug rehab classes. I was underage, I got youthful offender status, that wasn't my fault."

"I think you should have taken the whole rap."

"Are you insane? I would have served at least fifteen years. And it would not have gotten Janet off, she was still guilty of the stuff being at her house."

"I'm just saying, the drugs were yours and I think you should have said so."

"So this is what I'm coming home to, your judgment on me? Why is everything always my fault?" I started to cry. "Well, Dad, it's your fault Seely is dead, because you never loved her!"

"No, you're right, I didn't." His voice lowered. "She was a hard child to love. But don't you think I'm sorry, don't you think I'd do whatever I could to fix it?"

I was stunned. I never thought my father would admit to such a thing, I didn't even mean it when I said it.

"Well, Zack, don't you think I'm sorry too?"

"No, I don't."

"Fine, I'll just kill myself then!" I hung up on him feeling more lost than ever. Even my own father was against me.

One afternoon, Armando unexpectedly appeared at my door. He stood on my porch as finely dressed as ever with tears streaming down his face.

"Come in," I said. I closed the door and he grabbed me, hugging me tightly.

"Please, please forgive me, please, I didn't mean for her to die. I'm so sorry."

I held him, but said nothing.

After a few minutes, he asked to sit down. I offered him a chair. Seeing the boxes he said, "Are you moving?"

"Armando, why are you here?"

"I need you to believe I'm sorry."

"You lied in court."

"I had to, my lawyer said I had to, I didn't mean to hurt your family, I swear."

"Really? Then why not give me money now. Just pay the damages in cash."

"Negrita, the insurance gave them fifty thousand dollars, what more can they want?"

"Another fifty."

"I cannot, I just do not have it."

"Sure you don't, maricón. I made you that ten times over, but you only care about yourself. You're a thief, but it doesn't matter anymore. No amount of money can fix what you did."

"I know, I know, it is my fault, I am mierda."

"How many times did I tell you to slow down, how many? How many times did I say that you were going to kill someone?"

"Sí, sí, I know." He broke into fresh tears. "I ... *lo lamento todo.*"

"Yeah, and I guess you also regret setting me up?"

"Qué?"

"Ay cabrón. You tipped off that crooked cop, that's what I heard."

"*Nunca*! On my madre, I did not!"

"You don't even have a mother."

"I did not do it! And I didn't mean for Seely to ... to get hurt. It was a mistake." He looked down at the floor.

"You never mean it. All the suffering you cause, you're like, like, *el Diablo.*"

He put his face in his hands briefly, and then stood up. "Just say you believe that I am sorry. Por favor, por favor!"

"No, I can't."

He hung his head slightly and sighed, taking a deep breath. I opened the front door and he left. As he walked off, I saw that he had gotten a brand new red IROC-Z identical to the one Seely died in. I thought it was ghoulish.

"Don't you think you should have gotten black?" I called after him.

"Uh, por qué?"

"Black is a more appropriate color for a hearse." I slammed the door closed and sat down on the floor crying. I ached all over with regret; regret for everything I'd done, and for everything I'd not done.

I never saw Armando again.

Thirty-Five

I am stretched on your grave and will lie there forever,

If your hands were in mine, I'd be sure they'd not sever …

17th *Century Irish poem*

In January, I had gone to the complex where Seely and I lived the first half of our lives, to see the old landlady that knew me since before I was born.

"You know something strange, dear? The only empty apartment I have is the first one your parents lived in. You lived there too, until you were two and Seely was born." She patted my hand. "Then you all moved over to the next building, into the two bedroom."

When my father moved me in, he said, "Well, I'll be dammed. You know, this is where your mother and I spent our honeymoon night."

"When you get married at eighteen and you're three months pregnant, I guess renting an apartment comes before going on a trip, huh?"

"Yeah, it certainly does."

It was the smallest place I'd lived since I left home, but it was two rooms where I could lie about all day. And each night I could visit Seely, because she was buried in my father's family plot, only two miles away.

I didn't go at night because it was spooky. It wasn't. I played in old farm graveyards as a kid and I never found them scary. I went at night so no one would see me and declare me insane for lying on top of my sister's grave.

I took a blanket to the cemetery, tossed it over her burial plot, and lay down. I begged for her forgiveness, trying to converse with her through the earth that separated us.

I kept trying something I'd seen in an old occult rerun, maybe in One Step Beyond or The Twilight Zone. If a person dies and it is your fault, and they are innocent and you are bad, you can beg god wholeheartedly and god can make you swap places. God can take your life in place of theirs.

If it had worked, I would have gladly traded places with Seely. She had everything to live for, and I didn't deserve a future if she couldn't have one. She innocently followed me, the cool older sister, and I lead her to death. She was weaker than me, but she was kind and loving. I was ambitious and angry. She wanted kids and a family. I wanted money and glamour.

I tried for months, but the ritual produced no results. Seely stayed under the cool earth, and I woke up each day in my bed. I was never caught lying on her grave past midnight, begging god to release her from that casket and replace her saintly bones with my tainted ones. I once thought I had so much more than her: more bravery, more will, more strength, more brains. Now, I knew I had nothing over her. She had every warm human attribute I lacked, and the world needed her, not me.

I often thought of suicide, but I was afraid to hurt Zack. I thought he would die without me. Instead, I keened all day while blasting music to hide the sounds from the neighbors.

One day in early spring, I heard a car outside my apartment. I looked out to see three suits coming towards my door. They knocked. I was scared, but I figured whatever they had to say I might as well know now. So I opened my door halfway to talk to them.

"Yes, can I help you?" I said.

"I'm Agent Gimbal, and this is Agents Allen and Mitchell. We're here to talk to you."

"About what?"

"Well, we were wondering if you'd like to get some revenge on your ex-boyfriend?"

I opened the door wide, even though I was embarrassed that I looked like hell in an old sweat suit with no makeup, and my faced was blotched from crying.

"Please come in and sit down."

They sat on my luxurious drug-profit purchased living room set. I sat in a rocking chair facing them.

"Mind if I smoke?" Gimbal asked me.

I handed him an ashtray. "So, what police are you from?"

"We're FBI, Miss, and we want to put Armando away as long as possible. No one knows better than you how many people he's hurt. The DEA came to us. They can't ever get that man with drugs, you know how smart he is."

"Yes, I do."

"Well, they had the idea that we might want to get him on tax evasion, just to get him off the street, away from kids. Plus, we'll take away all the stuff he bought, you know, the cars, houses, boats. Michael told us that you could be our star witness. He said you spent a few years very close to Armando, and that you might know about his spending habits, his possessions, and the like."

"Michael, yes, please tell him I said hello ... he's right, I know quite a bit."

"Would you testify against Armando in a federal court of law? If he goes to trial, he could get twenty years and there's no parole in the federal prison system. It's just straight time."

"Yes, I would." I didn't even need to think about it.

The three of them came back the next two days and questioned me for many hours. They tape-recorded all of it. I answered every question truthfully except one. They asked me about Lalo, and I said I didn't know him. They insisted I'd been at his house in Miami, but I reminded them I was only there once, and I said that I waited in the entrance hall and met no one inside.

"You waited in a hall alone for six hours?" Agent Allen asked.

"Yeah, I read a book. I always carried a book in my purse, a lot of hanging with Armando involved waiting."

The agent glanced over at the wall, to where I had a large double set of bookcases stuffed with novels. He asked no more questions about anyone except Armando. I was relieved because I was talking to the federales only to give Armando a retaliatory strike, not to rat on some kingpin who would send a hit man after me. I didn't believe Armando would retaliate. He knew what he'd done to me. He knew the rules of engagement.

"Well, call me if you remember anything else," Gimbal said while handing me his card. He stood up to leave along with the other agents. "We'll let you know if we need you to come to court."

Months went by. No one called asking me to testify. I prayed they would. I dreamed of my revenge, picturing Armando desolate on a hard cot beneath the shadow of iron bars.

Finally I called Gimbal. With trembling fingers I pressed the numbers on my Trimline then balanced the receiver on my shoulder. My stomach tightened when I heard his phone ring.

"Armando took a plea, he's finished … his dealing days are done," Gimbal said.

"So what did he get?" I paced the room while my heart thumped.

"He's gonna do at least five years. We're also taking his property and stuff like I told you we would. Almost a million dollars worth."

I was silent. I had broken the code I'd sworn to live by and helped the federales. No matter the grounds I felt like a traitor.

Gimbal sensed my compunction and said, "Now you listen to me kid, you did the right thing."

But I got off the phone feeling defeated. My revenge felt hollow. Armando being imprisoned brought me no peace and it didn't change a thing. Seely was still dead.

I had cut all contact with everyone I knew from my former life as a drug queen. All I wanted was to somehow learn to live with Seely's death, which I felt was my fault. I didn't know then that learning to live with her death would mean spending decades trying to forgive myself for things I did and didn't do while she was alive.

I tried to focus on the future, taking courses at night in psychology and learning computers at my day job. I had no real goals, except to complete my probation without getting into trouble. I was terrified of returning to jail. I shuddered when thinking of my time there and I swore to myself I would do nothing that would ever cause me to end up there again. I became a model probationer, dutifully doing everything required of me, such as regular employment, weekly counseling, and regular drug testing. I went through an outpatient alcohol treatment program, after which I didn't take a single drink for the next fifteen years. I never touched drugs again. I was let off probation two years early for good behavior.

My life became simple. I spent my free time studying different spiritual philosophies through the theosophical society. I was no longer driven by a lust for money or glamour, or even by desperation to survive. Instead, I was filled with questions about life, death, and fate.

When I was released from probation, I quit my job and began a full-time search to find those answers. I soon found myself on a quest that led me away from my home, far from suburban New York, and far from the girl I once was.

Litanei

by

Johann Georg Jacobi

Rest in peace all souls
who have finished an anxious torment,
who have finished a sweet dream,
sated with life, born hardly,
from the world gone over departed:
all souls rest in peace!

Love full maiden souls,
whose tears not to be counted,
who a false friend have left
and the blind world disowned;
all, who from here have parted,
all souls rest in peace!

And those upon whom the sun never smiled
Beneath the moon on the thorns watched,
God, in the pure heavenly light
once to see in the face:
all, who from here have parted,
all souls rest in peace!

Afterword

I know little to nothing about most of the people in the book beyond the time the events took place. After Seely's death I left the area I had grown up in and never returned. I cut contact with everyone I had ever known and I've had no contact with anyone in my book since January 1986 except for my parents. They are on this list with people I was able to find out about through research. There were many people I could not find information about, partially because I knew very few people's last name and many people went by nicknames.

Armando: While writing this book I was shocked to find out that Armando never went to prison for tax evasion. Shortly after the FBI visited me the DEA caught him selling twenty pounds of cocaine a week. He became a prized informant for the DEA and was glowingly described as "cooperating substantially." The agent also said Armando was helping them apprehend major drug traffickers.

Two years later he was sentenced to four years in jail for repeated weapons offences. He was removed from jail the next day by federal agents and disappeared. He likely went into the federal witness protection program.

In total he spent one night in jail.

Carlos: Remains in prison serving a life sentence for murder.

Conner: Was later arrested for possession of a large quantity of cocaine. He went to prison for many years.

Joan: Remained with Stan minus a few stays in a battered women's shelter. He regularly threatens her life and physically abuses her. She maintains multiple restraining orders against him though they live in the same house. She never recovered from Seely's death.

Nikki: Nikki died in the early 90s for reasons unknown.

Zack: Lived a troubled life with many hardships. He remained in an unhappy marriage with Leona until he committed suicide, leaving six children behind. Four of them were still children aged nine through eighteen.

Leona: Inherited Zack's life insurance money. She sold their house and abandoned all of their children, moving away with an estimated half a million dollars. Various relatives took in most of Zack's children.

Acknowledgments

I'd like to thank my editor, Daniel, for his dedication to this project, his generosity of time, and his ability to translate my Spanglish. I could never have written this book without him.

And Jeffrey, who helped me turn a pile of loose notes into an outline, and later into a manuscript. Without his coaching, teaching, and encouragement, this book would not exist.

Thanks to Daniel and Michael for their invaluable research, advice, and guidance.

And thanks to Colleen and Ariel for support that made this book possible.

I'd also like to thank Julia for eagerly reading each chapter as it was completed, and for giving me excellent feedback on each one. I'm also grateful to Allae, Matthew, Ken, Hrana, Dave, and others who read the book and encouraged me to publish it.

I am thankful to Richard, Mr. D, and Gram, who got me addicted to books as a child.

Finally, I want to thank M, whose caring changed my life forever.

CPSIA information can be obtained
at www.ICGtesting.com
Printed in the USA
FSHW011632040920
73568FS

9 781468 199246